THE CYNICAL EDUCATOR

Ansgar Allen

may f l y
www.mayflybooks.org

First published by MayFlyBooks in paperback in Leicester and free online at www.mayflybooks.org in 2017.

CC: Ansgar Allen 2017

Images by Frances Allen, University of California, Berkeley.

Cover design by Zanna Allen

ISBN (Print) 978-1-906948-35-1
ISBN (PDF) 978-1-906948-36-8

This work is licensed under the Creative Commons Attribution- Noncommercial-No Derivative Works 4.0 Unported. To view a copy of this license, visit http://creativecommons.org/licenses/by-nc- nd/3.0/ or send a letter to Creative Commons, 171 Second Street, Suite 300, San Francisco, California, 94105, USA.

Detail from a Dead Fly - Back

ABOUT THE AUTHOR

Ansgar Allen is a Lecturer in Education at the University of Sheffield and author of *Benign Violence: Education in and beyond the Age of Reason*.

CONTENTS

I	DEAD MATERIALS	1

I am Culture
On Pedantry
On Writing

II	PROMISED GOODS	13

Glorify What Exists
Our Nihilism
Half Dead Already

III	BENEVOLENT EDUCATORS	33

The Great Educational Swindle
A Christian Soul
Sin Multiplied

IV	OUR EDUCATIONAL CONSCIENCE	59

The Healthy Educator
Principles of Pastoral Care
Educational Ill-Health
Principles of Educational Sickness

V	MASS CYNICISM	81

Emptied Out and Set to Work
Our Detached Negativity
The Educator's Smile
The Educator's Last Hope
The Educator's Last Breath

VI	INSULTS AND OBSCENITIES	105

Scandalous Teachings
Bawdy Educators
Educated Bodies
A Returned Diogenes

VII	SPIRIT OF HEAVINESS	133

Held in Denial
Sade as Educator
Mastery or Failure

VIII	A MODERN FETISH	151

Incessant Motion
As Universal Good
The Educated Critic
An Odd Beast Indeed
Consumptive Educators

IX	THE ABSURD	171

Artificial Brutalities
The Tragedy of Education
With Blistered Fingers
Absurd Lessons

I

DEAD MATERIALS

I am Culture[1]
Our educators declare: Education is dying all around us. They act cornered. As they fight for education they fight for us. They fight for civilization itself. 'Human history becomes more and more a race between education and catastrophe', say the educated, and blink.[2] But when they fly, or tumble as if out of a barrel, education and catastrophe are hand-in-hand, overturning, downturning.

*

Dying all about us? It hardly lived. But education is vital, cry the educated. *More* education – of whatever kind – remains the only conceivable remedy.[3]

*

Aspire to be more like us, say the educated. You may have what we have had. You may hope to be as educated as the best of us. So resist us. Become us.

*

Education is not perverted, it is perversion. Education sets down the intellectual and affective foundations for another century of rampant growth, exploitation, pollution and barbarity. The educator helps model the directionless, frantic subjectivity we too must acquire. Education sets us up so that we are already defeated by it. Education prepares our defeat by constructing frameworks of disappointment. It develops terminal subjectivities so we are forever dependent on its life-support, so we may live as if part deceased. Here, Cynic and Cynical educator serve to cultivate our misgivings, dredging impressions from unimpressionable minds. No proofs are offered. We are not convinced through painstaking argument or reasoned debate that our educational ideals are unjustified, and perhaps unjustifiable. They discredit themselves. Our beliefs are abandoned as we struggle to take them in earnest. The Cynic seeks not assent but your complicity.

*

There is a difference between the Cynic's point of view and everyday cynicism, though the Cynic may still appeal to the latter. Everyday cynicism prepares you well, the Cynic may say, but requires adjustment. Confined to a lowercase 'c', this cynicism exists in a weakened state, reactive and conditional.

*

To be a better cynic you are directed to the Cynics of yore.[4] A barbed invitation, for borrowings are fraught with difficulty. After two millennia straightforward emulations are out of the question. You would not bring forth a returned Diogenes. He would not squat before you and deliver a lesson in Cynic contempt. Some tried but shat for cinematic effect, exchanging one aperture for another.[5]

*

A Cynicism of our own might still be attempted. A militant philosophy promoting change through personal discomfort. With it we give way to our suspicions. We confront educational subjectivities as systems of bad faith. We encounter educational frameworks that bind us still, though they are frayed and torn between themselves. A Cynicism of our own pays close attention to cynical attitudes otherwise lost in the day-to-day of work and living. It roots them out, transforms them and performs them to greater effect. It draws attention to the presence of everyday cynicism, nowhere more entrenched, and at times nowhere more disavowed, than in education. This cynicism becomes manifest in our grumblings, but cloaks itself too. Our cynicisms are tied just as much to moments of romance and hope, where nothing is more assured and fondly believed than the promise education makes over and never delivers. To be cynical today is to live with paradox, half-formed and fretful.

*

The educated are cynics in a more personal sense. This cynicism becomes manifest in the standing of educated people, in the straight-backed conceit of the educated person. Even more as they stride out. Their gait may be distinct, but is assumed and maintained by little more than habit. Educated people are doomed in modernity to a spinning of culture from their entrails.[6] Finally driven to cry out: 'I am culture, *I am!*'[7] Peevish and uptight, educated people feel this to be so, but refuse to admit theirs is a performance like any other. Our modern cynicism is found everywhere then, including where we least expect. It drains where it might invigorate.

*

This book takes aim at you and me, at our cynical attachments to education and the educated person. It unearths the teacher within us. It confronts us with our disavowed cynicisms only to affirm them. It traces the origins of everyday cynicism by locating the rise of cynicism in the fall of Western education. The romantic educator – that last bastion of the Western educational experience – is now falling from grace, though with a death rattle that may last decades still. Education is under attack more than ever for failing to deliver on its promises, but rarely doubted itself. Few see how its failures are systematically produced, and necessary.

*

The death of education? Announced last century more than once, proclaimed without conviction and forgotten.[8] Insist on the question mark because education remains. We may suffer its last agonies, our vision clouded by its pain. But we continue as educators and educated people. A little flushed. Rather listless. Possessive. Prancing back and forth upon a grave we refuse to acknowledge. Last rites have no function. Only a Dionysian wake will disturb our slumber as we imbibe our sorrow and encounter what we already inter.[9] Struggling to remember, we ache with a loss of which we can hardly speak.

On Pedantry
With every extinguished life histories are lost, completing that lifelong attrition of memories which fade and alter. We refuse to admit the world is 'draining itself' of places, events and memories, most of which are never heard nor described. [10] Our histories are made of fragments. Transformed in their descent, augmented with chunks of our present. It is laughable but symptomatic we insist on finding order and support in our past. Our pedantry prevents us from standing back only to discover we are already fallen.

*

Amid educated people, academics are specialist pretenders. If this were a more standard text, it would disguise itself as commentary; as a history chastened to its timeframe; a philosophy limited to its field. This text would announce itself as an elucidation of Nietzsche, or Foucault, or some other late modern canon. It would expend itself recounting positions one might take with regard to their work. It would make substantive claims that others may then contest. It would locate itself within a proliferating field of study beneath which both are submerged, and would do so by default and without a second thought. For that is how academics operate, paying due regard to their kin. When I appeal to the work of another, I do so without the roll of a drum. This convention – insisting you reference a good slice of your contemporaries – exercises more scholarly restraint than it offers assistance. It functions as a condition of entry. Academics reference one another because they defy anything remotely original to announce itself as such. Material of this kind takes too long to digest. Nobody has time or energy for that, not even your traditional academic whose peristaltic motions could win records for lethargy. But original work remains the obsession. The ancient code whereby 'originality is a defect, innovation is suspect, and fidelity to tradition, a duty' is long dismissed.[11] Our academic code insists we parade back and forth under a banner. It declares our commitment to fresh ideas, new insights and innovations. In practice this pledge inverts. It manifests as an obsession with all that remains unoriginal in each text. Academia is as preoccupied with its fetish for originality as it is suspicious of its appearance. Academics need to be assimilated. So this pursuit of originality – by which each writer attempts a position against the heavy bibliography he or she must employ – leads to a profound and tightly felt academic bondage. Which gives another slant on the joke: I've seen the best research ideas of my generation destroyed by a brief literature search.[12]

*

We might relate to texts differently.[13] Each book, each treatise considered an accumulation of dead materials. Each had its motion, logic of advance and now lifeless inertia. We grasp hold, tear along for a while, and grasp another. Grabbing texts when writing one's own acquires its own momentum; live for an instant, dead the next. Least pleasurable mode of transport: the philosophical disquisition. Riding to no effect, one falls asleep.

*

The Cynic's dead materials were organised as sayings (*chreiai*) and provocations to awaken the living. But they were open to adjustment too. Concerted attempts were made to idealize Cynicism, as Roman Stoic philosophers traced a line of descent from Socrates, through Cynicism, to themselves. The educated wit also claimed the tradition as his own, transforming it into a literary genre.[14] The force of Cynicism, a lived philosophy that debunks convention, insults decorum, mocks philosophy and undermines pretension, was thereby reduced. This philosophy of deviant life, as scornful as it was devoted to humanity, is all but lost to history. Scholars may well remind us that Cynicism once took a more bawdy form. We may learn how the first Cynics bore witness to their philosophy by obscene gestures and scatological acts. But we can hardly fathom why. We cannot understand ancient Cynicism without cheapening it or turning it into respectable philosophy.

On Writing

The academic who goes cap in hand to the publishing house, begging to be considered profitable, needs approval like a rat needs petting. Better to bite the hand that pats. It scarcely even feeds. These folk are so well fed already.

*

'This book raises more problems than it answers' – a common refrain amongst authors. It defers to the reader in hope of better reception. Fortunately such deferrals, deceptions and seductions can be dispensed with here. The problems of this book are raised as one does the devil.

*

'This book provides no systematic answers; it makes no claim to be definitive' – the scholar's excuse for inaction.

*

'Everything is dangerous'[15] – 'nothing can be trusted'. The mantra of radical scholars trained to suspect power and intrigue everywhere. At most, those insisting power always eludes analysis, that definitive critique is a hopeless dream, offer the following: Recommending little, prescribing naught, they oppose nothing definitively, merely outlining a 'horizon and a background upon which we may move with care'.[16] But their modesty is deceptive. It generates a 'dogmatism of the impasse' much 'harder to root out than dogmatic conviction'.[17] Expressed as a kind of vigilance, as a determined effort to be prudent in one's statements, avoiding any which appears overly certain of itself, this high intellectualism has 'flattened out contemporary thought' under its scrupulous yet heavy tread.[18] These radicals of the impasse celebrate the virtues of intellectual caution and scholarly calculation that have, we cannot help but notice, the convenient effect of justifying their continued employment. There is always another problem to describe and paper to write. Our challenge is more demanding than a call to perpetual vigilance. It is to live at times without caution, even without calculation.

*

This book seeks out its populace with polemic intent. It was not written for applause. Some academics would be received in this fashion, reaching out with a generosity of spirit born of conceit. The civilizing mission of the profession enchants those who fervently believe in accessibility before all else. Those seeking to *excite* their public will also dupe it into believing that the university, and this academic in particular, is indispensible. Those wishing to *inspire* their public conjure a populace that eagerly awaits each offering. This simplistically deferential, peaceable citizenry is the kind of illusion upon which academic public engagement depends. But the university most often greets its public like a damp squib, losing sparkle amid widespread indifference. The university machine (which must secure the reputation of the institution before all else) grasps on to small pockets of enthusiasm it misreads and misrepresents as an affirmation of its kindly mission. All window-dressing and good feeling is tied up, in other words, with a form of institutional inertia, where large corporations adapt to changing circumstance by managing their image rather than questioning their content.

*

Academic writing will not become open to others so long as it perpetuates the tedious rituals of the craft. Once described as the 'most eccentric latecomer of all philosophical forms',[19] the peer-reviewed paper has academia in its grip. That academic thought has confined itself to single slabs of writing – where all that can be expressed is that which can be enclosed within a prescribed word limit with all the structural, stylistic, topical and hence intellectual constraints this involves – is one of the most remarkable and noteworthy of the uncontested assumptions that make up academic discourse. Academics are not unaware of other styles of writing, and feel the constraints of their discipline rather acutely when work is rejected for publication. But conformity is at a high premium. Work must be adapted and resubmitted if the academic is to remain 'research active'. Indeed our very conception of research has been reduced to that which is funded, published, and ranked. All else is defined by what it lacks. It is unpublished research. Unranked, unfunded, perhaps even unfundable.

*

Against the stifling conformity of a profession in which 'transgressors' have their journals too – inflicting just another code upon those who must publish or otherwise perish, establishing yet another cartel where people of similar taste gather together for protection – the 'unhoused mind' does not seek recognition and applause, and hence admission as a condition of existence.[20] Like Diogenes the Cynic, whose existence on the social and institutional periphery bore witness to its perverse construction, those labouring at this periphery are prepared to be consistently misread, just as today's homeless are misunderstood by social workers whose conception of a positive outcome is the product of a 'housed' state of mind.[21] Attempts to work against the boundaries of academic life are similarly misunderstood and misapprehended, or apprehended and despised. They are tolerated only as caricatures of deviance, as part of a wider liberal fetish which finds solace in its benevolent gestures. 'How open we are,' these liberals declare, 'since we tolerate your existence'.

*

A reading of the playwright Bertolt Brecht would have academics better alienate their audience. In so doing, they would also alienate themselves, from their work. For Brecht, enchanted publics make passive audiences, disappearing and reappearing within the spectacle, identifying with its narrative. Against this tendency, Brecht would remind his audience and have his actors remind themselves of its material presence, of the distance between audience and play, actor and lines. By extension, when the university reaches out it would instruct the public on how it ordinarily excludes them, and remind the academic of the oddities and exclusions of academic life. Rather than invite the public to engage with the university and be at one with it in spirit, the addressed public would be encouraged to distance itself from the university it confronts. Academic writing, so influenced, would not condescend to its readers by inviting its audience with gentle encouragement into the 'deep knowledge' of the text. Rather, academic writing would encourage a degree of ironic detachment and suspicion, even estrangement from itself.

*

Friedrich Nietzsche will at times repel even his most avid supporters. His intent, so he tells us, was not to 'intoxicate' his audience and 'force it to the height of a moment of strong and elevated feeling'. Such audiences have already 'been whipped too much' into 'aping the high tide of the soul!' ... 'What now?' Nietzsche asks: 'One gives the mole wings and proud conceits – before it is time to go to sleep, before he crawls back into his hole? One sends him to the theatre and places large glasses before his blind and tired eyes?' 'That is decent,' you say; 'that is entertaining; that is culture...' But our mole has been distracted, quite deliberately. And besides, 'whoever finds enough tragedy and comedy in himself, probably does best when he stays away from the theatre. Or if he makes an exception, the whole process, including the theatre, the audience, and the poet, will strike him as the really tragic or comic spectacle, while the play that is performed will mean very little to him by comparison.' We might turn then, with Nietzsche, away from the 'narcotica' of 'so-called higher culture', and confront the tragi-comic nature of our daily existence.[22] By making mischief with 'the habits of our senses',[23] by working with form as well as content, Nietzsche confronts his reader with meditations as untimely as they are upsetting of conventional mores. Nietzsche's writings do not accommodate themselves to the reader. The reader is forced to confront the space between maxims that insist, at each break, not to become comfortable with the tone, conventions and style of the text. The reader should become, and remain distressed.

*

Educators may become distressed, and feel the torment of their profession, but are rarely shaken from it. Educators are instead stirred into action, as if they could save education from itself. But education itself goes unquestioned. Indeed a radical questioning of education is ruled out by the common insistence it be saved before all else. So when you hear echoes of their refrain, 'Save us! Save education! Arise!' Hear too the Cynic reply: 'Arise what?'

*

This book takes aim at the conceit of educated people, in particular those educated educators in the business of educating others. They believe an educational good to exist and defend it against attack. The good of the educational good is assumed everywhere and without question. Precisely here their conceit resides – a conceit which is yours and mine. On all fours, this book sets off. It confronts the educated with their downgoing.

*

A new breed of Cynic trots forth: The challenge it declares, is to be 'both philosopher and fool, moralist and rogue'[24] as we engage in the patient, urgent labour conjured for us, and demanded of us by none other than our educated nihilism.

II

PROMISED GOODS

Glorify What Exists
Despite all corruptions the inherent goodness of education is believed incorruptible. This conviction will not be abandoned however much education is debased, reduced to the status of commodity, or instrument for 'getting ahead'. Despite everything that degrades education, supplying endless source material for its critics, the romance of an educational good lives on. Even those claiming to have seen it all, those who have become cynically detached and will no longer be disappointed, fall under its spell. Through tears of pain or with eyes dried blank, educators remain enamoured. They 'glorify what exists' for fear of its dissolution.[1]

*

In today's educational circles, those holding to the remnants of twentieth century progressivism believe the worst kind of educator asserts himself as a purveyor of expertise. To privilege one's expertise, with the implication that the educator's primary mission is to transmit this knowledge to the student who must listen attentively, is viewed as if it were a perfect demagoguery to be driven out of the classroom by all means. Our last surviving progressives rail against such expressed authority as symptomatic of a lack of openness to the knowledge of others. Such educators are at their purest when beginning each lesson with the utterance: 'I am here to facilitate your learning, I will learn from you as you learn'. The alternative and opposite introduction: 'Here is what you must know', is only expressed under duress when teaching to the test. Meanwhile educators and commentators of a reactionary persuasion rage against this 'progressive orthodoxy' that somehow, they claim, remains alive and well despite the devastatingly effective work of their predecessors to bring it to its knees. Denouncing that spectre, they assert the virtue of the teacher's classroom sovereignty and the value of a lesson that begins: 'Now I will tell you what is worth knowing'. As familiar as it is tiresome, this endless dispute over whether or not the teacher is a tyrant to exercise authority in the classroom, endless debate considering the justifiable limits and scope of teacherly influence, operates as if a non-tyrannical teacher could, with compassion, strip education of its barbarities. Here manifests a conceit common to all parties, a shared belief that education could be rescued from the effects of power, either by removing or by justifying the presence of the overbearing teacher; as if this would allow the essential 'goodness' of the teacher-educator to be realised at last before us. This shared conceit took modern form as it became attached to the idea that any single individual, suitably trained, might achieve the kind of reasonable and dependable neutrality expected of today's educator. Few today could still defend this position in good faith. We late moderns are most of us far too cynical for that. Yet we remain attached to its echo, out of weakness and for want of alternative.

Our Nihilism

Western educators cry out, suffering the effects of their 'European nihilism'.[2] There is something consumptive, in the tubercular sense, about today's educator. Riven by a disease which becomes manifest in the wasting away of high ideals, the educator hides blood-filled sputum in a rag. Once waved aloft, now filled with detritus. In it we find denial, the pursuit of distraction, and over-attachment to defeated ideals. Three lines of catarrh. These remnants constitute education today.

*

Embrace your nihilism with tears and laughter for 'the biggest laughs are based on the biggest disappointments'.[3] The hardest laugh and also the most difficult, is for those still insisting on their optimism.[4] As the 'destiny of two millennia of Western history' nihilism is our unavoidable affliction.[5] Those educators claiming to exist beyond its reach merely deny its presence. Those hoping to alter its destiny make only noise. There is no quick and easy escape. We are trapped in the digestive tract of Western history. Our challenge, perhaps our only option, is to contrive an 'accomplished nihilism'.[6] Here is no wish to supersede modernity, or supersede education. Accomplished nihilism admits its predecessors as its facts of existence. It decides to interrogate rather than ignore its past, realising it remains haunted. The nihilist can only hope to 'dissolve modernity [and dissolve education] through a radicalization of its own constitutive tendencies'.[7] Hence Zarathustra's commandment: 'What falleth, that shall one also push!'[8] The accomplished nihilist desires only to force one out.

*

We follow education downwards giving its 'worst' aspects their due. And once we have stared into the educational abyss, having chased education to the bottom of its despair. After our Cynicism has taken us into the darkness that education prepared. As we face the stench of its defeated ideals and aborted lives, we must attempt, indeed learn to breathe in its ruins. Written for consumptives, for those already fallen ill, this book would have educated folk better cough, expectorate and spit.[9]

*

Spit furthest at the promise of hope – at the assurance we might with assistance overcome our nihilism. From habit we would have ourselves 'sustained by a hope which cannot be refuted by any actuality – which is not *done away with* by any fulfilment: a hope in the Beyond'.[10] But nihilism is not refuted by appeal. When nihilism is denounced, its consequences are mistaken for the thing itself. We do not perceive nihilism as a cultural bequeathment 'whose essential ground lies in metaphysics'.[11] Nihilism was established as a framework of appeal: as the world was given meaning and denied sense by reverence to something beyond sensory perception. As each transcendental order and system of appeal was contested, refined, augmented, corrupted, debased and replaced, frantic attempts were made to restore meaning to the universe. Becoming most apparent during times of upheaval, nihilism is denounced as if it were a temporary condition.

Declarations against nihilism, claims it can be overcome, generally remain captive to a 'logic of development' that is built into European thought. 'Overcoming' is inscribed in a tradition of thought for which 'the new is identified with value through the mediation of the recovery and appropriation of the foundation-origin.'[12] The claim that we might overcome our nihilism falls prey to a similar drive, one that attempts to establish a new basis of legitimacy by staging a recovery, rebirth, or return to, foundational systems of value. In the Nietzschean tradition, these foundational hopes are radically interrogated, with origins unveiled as moments that only receive homage from afar, for the closer you come to an origin, the more it flattens out into a sequence of events: *'The more insight we possess into an origin the less significant does the origin appear'.*[13] If we retain our commitment to origins, this commitment remains unsatisfied, because origins always retreat into the 'background of the already begun'.[14] We are faced with strange continuities and repeated eruptions. Doubting origins, we develop a suspicion of the 'new' as a continuation of the old – where the new generally acquires the old as a confused inheritance. This is the history of nihilism, a history of new values becoming old, and old values becoming new.

*

Our self-told destiny murmurs on as we open out the triptych of Western history. For Christianity 'history appears as the history of salvation', only to become 'the search for a worldly condition of perfection, before turning, little by little, into the history of progress'.[15] This latter formation is uniquely diminished, finding its ultimate purpose to be in creating conditions in which further progress is possible. Our nihilism is expressive of this triptych; it represents our disappointment with the third panel and its superficial illustrations, in contrast to the glory of those to which they are hinged.

*

For some the advent of Western nihilism is not to be regretted. As we suffer its catastrophic effects, we gain access to 'the process of becoming of the 'false' constructs of metaphysics, morality, religion and art' – and education. This catastrophe brings into view 'the entire tissue of erring that alone constitutes the wealth or, more simply put, the *essence* of *reality*.'[16] Those turning away in search of security, grasping for fundamentals, do not merely deny themselves this perception, they set out in search of new masters.

*

The accomplished nihilist resists the "pathos of authenticity' or in Nietzschean terms...resistance to the accomplishment of nihilism' which surrounds us today.[17] From this point of view, other cultures, subcultures, and oppressed groups are not by their former or continued exclusion more authentic. Nor are marginalised research methodologies, modes of representation, or neglected forms of participation more legitimate than the traditional approaches they hope to replace. Such attempts to find value, authenticity and direction in anything suppressed are symptomatic of a weakened nihilism, retreating from the abyss of its making. Active nihilism does not ground its hope in the subaltern but confronts itself with the effects of mainstream culture in decline.

*

But we have been schooled too well and too long to unlearn our lessons without struggle. By habit we insist there be hope, that nihilism will not run its course. We will find value and meaning somewhere before all is said and done. Divined in ancient Greece; we have been educated to follow in step. The first philosophical schools taught their members to ration existence to a higher ideal, to an ideal beyond achievement and beyond question. We remain haunted by this schematic. Distinctly unphilosophical as they have become, our schools are still harried by the educational figure of Socrates. His was an educational scheme where a quest to give meaning to one's existence was yoked to an experience of doubt, and a promise too, that education would be its overcoming. It was necessary to learn first of all to be guided by this promise. Belief in the promise of education was a prerequisite for one's subordination to it. Henceforth, the educated were those ready to proceed before the fact. They were the credulous.

*

Socrates goaded others, but claimed to be himself driven by an inner daemon or divine voice that issued signs as warnings.[18] Perhaps here can be found an early version of your 'moral conscience'.[19] First installed by Socratic inquisition; developed through educational activities designed to raise doubt in the individual about his or her worth and understanding. These techniques would teach us to relate differently (and with suspicion) to the self. They would install our conscience by a procedure, the malice of which was concealed by its benign educational intent. The good news is we can blame our education. Indeed what is education for but to furnish us with our excuses? The bad news is the excuses keep coming.

*

Make no mistake, our conscience may be ancient in pedigree, perhaps even a little decrepit, but remains dangerously effective with a grasp tightened by centuries. By it we acquired a soul, as the body develops rigor mortis — a temporary stiffening, which departs as decomposition begins. The more educated we became the more it calcified, inflicting its regimen upon us. With it we are encumbered by a whole load of weighty, solemn materials passed down from history. In part a pre-modern device, the product of an era many today would locate far behind (and below) that ideal to which they still aspire: a modern, enlightened sensibility.

Half Dead Already

Education is best attacked as it is venerated, by tracing it to some cradle of Western civilization. In Plato's dialogues we find education modelled as a relationship demanding trust and deferred gratification. We discover that Socrates (our first and best model teacher) does not educate directly but relentlessly interrogates, basing his replies on those things each pupil 'admits that he himself knows.' These things become those articles of faith each pupil must be induced to doubt.[20] Socrates develops an educational art, in other words, one that operates by seduction.[21] The pupil is enticed to willingly engage, discourse openly, and remain available to adjustment. The educational challenge is to turn away from sensory distraction. The best pupil in such a scheme is he who is most easily seduced by education, he who already believes in the educational good promised by the educational encounter.

*

The Socratic teacher builds so much on so little, relying on foundations of professed ignorance, guided by the unfolding structure of his interrogations. The tremendous leap of faith implied here is striking. Surely to teach through ignorance and dialogue alone would be too much for us now; it would be a weight our conscience could not bear. What if on occasion Socrates did more damage than good, unsettling his pupils assuredly, yet generating little of value in return? But these are matters of concern for today's educator. The Socratic conscience was less stirred; it was daemonic and occasional. Socrates was free of that constant, nagging presence, our modern voice of guilt, which echoes the pained worldview of its Christian forbears. Unlike its distant Socratic ancestor, this conscience requires something rather more concrete than a leap of faith to justify its interventions and submissions. Our contemporary educational conscience no longer abides mere dialogue and suggestion. It requires an institutional framework for reassurance; it insists on its own confinement. Today we demand some kind of norm, some sort of procedure, some conception of outcomes, some shared sense of technique, to be settled. And even then we remain disturbed.

*

Centuries after Plato yet to our eyes still ancient, Plotinus offers some measure of reassurance to the baffled educator. He adapts Platonism by outlining a path of sorts to guide those seeking wisdom. The spiritual progress of his imagined philosopher-pupil was divided into a number of stages, beginning with exercises to detach the soul from the impulses of the body, and ending with full though transient union with a supreme, undivided transcendental entity known as 'the One'. But this educational sequence, affording a structure of sorts and a vague outline of progression, would not instruct the pupil directly. The educational path could not be rationalised. And its object remained ineffable. Such an education relied upon indirect instruction through a sequence of analogies and negations, still requiring in other words a leap of faith.[22] More clearly sequenced perhaps, yet still too vague for us now. There is no reassurance here for a modern educational conscience that requires far more than analogies and negations. Demanding the support of definite procedures and finding such guidance readily available, this conscience is attached to more proximal objectives. These objectives have been reduced in turn so as to ignore, forget, and yet repeat unwittingly in a frenzied but shadowy form the ancient philosophical quest for wisdom. In our more utilitarian age, educational objectives have been collected together like so many nuts and bolts.[23]

*

To encounter education in its pre-modern contexts, abandon those sensibilities which govern not only how education is practiced but also how education is felt. Relinquish your subjective attachments and become cold to the educational endeavour. More distorting than any other is that warmth of feeling we associate with the educational conscience which insists upon the goodness of education before all else. To paraphrase Nietzsche, this is how the educational beast in us wants to be lied to.[24] It would have us believe that education can be genuine and morally pure, that it can exist as a moment of simple generosity where good intentions become synonymous with good deeds. Without this belief the everyday violence of education would be too great to bear. We would find ourselves unable to endure its presence, despite its distribution (and concealment thereby) across artifices weighing so evenly we become convinced of their necessity. Without that conscience, with it finally relinquished, no artifice will suffice to conceal the violence, even the benign violence, of the educational endeavour. So become cold, educate and be educated without clothing yourself against the chill.

*

From cadaver to cosmic vacuum, Western education draws us down by degrees. We are rendered numb, duped into experiencing extreme cold as if it were heat, as if we could be warmed by that cosy, promising, promised space of an educational good. We will not see how coldly education inherits its point of view, denigrating our orb in favour of another, putting down this life for the promise of one higher (or better). With unflagging commitment, debased educational realities are contrasted to ineffable educational goods. And by unwitting obedience to its precepts, we are as disturbed – scandalised – by educational failure, as we are perpetually committed to the idea that failure must occur.

*

Platonic idealism may be attacked, but is only half our inheritance. There is another argument for education. It claims Aristotelian roots but is similarly judgemental. The inherent goodness of education is not made impossible by its failure to match up against pre-given forms – that would be our Platonic inheritance. Rather, the inherent failure of education to objectify its goodness is a product of its pursuit: the Aristotelian argument.

*

Some would have us return to Aristotle's notion of *praxis*, though it is feared we have all but lost the capacity for it. As a form of practical reasoning, praxis is acquired (and manifested) on the job. Praxis cannot be pre-defined, decided externally, or set down in writing, since it defines itself via a process of reflection that 'reflexively changes the 'knowledge-base' which informs it'.[25] The ends or aims of praxis are 'inseparable from, and intrinsic to, praxis and can only exist in praxis itself'.[26] Though the ends, means and indeed norms of praxis are locally defined, praxis remains high-minded enough in its commitments, seeking to realise that great philosophical simper known as the 'good life'. That life does not exist as something which can be theoretically specified in advance, nor can it be objectively realised. The nature of the good life only becomes known through praxis. Outside its realm of action one cannot judge whether or not it has been reached because the good life is only ever manifested in action. It consists in how we respond to particular situations and scenarios in all their temporal uniqueness. Certain activities allow us to realise the good inherent to human existence, others do not – highly technical activities would be in the latter category. Education is or at least ought to be in the former, insofar as its practitioners constantly negotiate its conditions of existence. Educators orient themselves by on-going negotiation to the good that is inherent in their work. Indeed that good, the good of education, becomes something that one 'has to do' because it can only be realised in action.[27] For the good of education to warrant pursuit, it must be assumed that educational practice can realise, in and of itself, a morally worthwhile form of human life. Building on this assumption educators must know their primary objective is to accomplish the educational potential, the inherent goodness, of each educational moment through praxis. Under these conditions and none other, educators will set about practicing or hoping to practice the good life that education promises. Driven by a desire for what is 'worthwhile', where that which is worthwhile can only be judged in action, the educator is 'guided by a moral disposition to act truly and justly', a quality the Greeks called *phronesis*.[28] Phronesis functions as a guiding virtue, and like everything else must be acquired through practice. Educational practice is concerned, then, not only with realising the inherent goodness of education, but with cultivating the virtue, or disposition to do good, of the educational practitioner. But as a practical endeavour, which constantly adjusts as conditions change, the quest for a good life (a life that is objectively or independently unassailable) must be constantly undertaken... These ideas have some resonance, even now. It becomes apparent that education is not only beholden to a Platonic promise which haunts it still and returns in ever more perverse forms. Education is subject to an Aristotelian equivalent – with a similar afterlife.[29] The Aristotelian position claims that education is promissory in and of itself. Educational practice is a pursuit based on a promise made by educators when educating. Never to be objectified, it is the hope of each passing moment.

*

Education is given the idea that 'man always encounters the good in the form of the particular'. It is for the person acting to 'know and decide, and he cannot let anything take this responsibility from him'.[30] The Aristotelian argument for education places responsibility here, with the educator, and with the student too. Indeed, the 'person listening to Aristotle's lecture' should not expect to receive what the philosopher cannot provide. The student 'must be mature enough' not to ask that 'his instruction provide anything other than it can and may give'.[31] It is a sign of the recipient's maturity to understand that the philosopher cannot teach us how to educate or how to be educated as if it were a skill, nor can he objectify the inherent good of education. That good is realised in the moment, it lives and dies by the moment. The 'basis of moral knowledge', he discovers, is a situated thing, revealed only to those who seek it out in praxis.[32] The educator's moral bearing is his unique achievement, a product of each passing moment. As such nobody can assay it, or take it from him. His commitment to the educational good is his pursuit of an ideal located in practice. If you want to objectify that ideal and locate the educational good, you must take it from his cold dead hand. Or so this educator might say, in a moment of heightened feeling. Become inactive, you will find it turned to dust.

*

For Plato we are already so much dust, being too earthly to begin with. So the lesson is different: 'The best philosopher is a dead philosopher; the best educator is a dead educator.' These are not expressions of contempt. In the perverse view of Platonic philosophy they venerate philosopher and educator alike. This tradition treats the 'world of the living' as if it were a 'phenomenal shell'.[33] We are trapped, it declares, prevented from accessing a kind of philosophical truth that exists beyond sense perception. Considered thus, death does not upset philosophy. Death is the affliction of bodies alone. Bodies are those sad temporary prisons to which we are confined. Our intellects are better homed elsewhere, in the eternal realm of thought.[34] The ancient philosopher of this cast of mind welcomes death as liberation, for life only makes philosophy difficult. The philosopher may enjoy this life in a manner of his own, but what the philosopher cannot stand is the unphilosophical life. A life of *that* kind is manifestly not worth living; a prejudice the educated inherit. A life without education is a life without worth.

*

On the eve of execution our first and best model educator affirmed his condition, as one disciple laughingly put, it of being 'half dead already'.[35] Defining death quite simply 'as the release of the soul from the body',[36] and philosophy as the rejection of bodily distractions such as food, drink and sex, as a turning away from the body and towards the soul in pursuit of wisdom; Socrates claimed that the true philosopher already frees himself 'from association with the body (so far as is possible)' and so has little to fear from death.[37] Since 'true philosophers make dying their profession',[38] anyone 'distressed at the prospect of dying' is no lover of wisdom, and no philosopher.[39] He is trapped by the love of his body. The body is his diversion. It prevents the soul from achieving that clarity of perspective from which it reasons best. Human affairs in general – more often affairs of the body and its passions than affairs of the mind – begin to appear 'awfully puny' from the perspective of the death-bound philosopher.[40] Death becomes a welcome opportunity. Those awaiting death must occupy their time in anticipation. They require an education in mortification.[41]

*

At most philosophy would offer a 'foretaste' of wisdom.[42] Despite variation between schools and philosophies (Epicurean, Stoic, Sceptic, Platonist, Aristotelian), each recommended its own system of life-denial. Each had its own regimen attached to a decidedly untouchable notion of the philosophical, and hence educational good it offered. Each insisted on a kind of deference to the love (*philos*) of wisdom (*sophia*), whereby a philosopher only ever tends towards wisdom – it can only be approximated, never achieved. Unlike the sage whose divine insights are inspired rather than reasoned, the philosopher is reasoned but rarely inspired.[43] The educational message is clear: 'You will orient yourself towards wisdom but forever remain in its shadow'. Philosophy, and hence education, are defined by what they lack – that is, by a norm which escapes them.[44] The Socratic teacher, whose superiority is guaranteed by the admission he is wise because he knows he is not, occupies an ambiguous position here, being neither quite of this world, nor quite outside it. This teacher points the way towards wisdom without having to objectively achieve or embody it. This teacher is nothing more, and nothing less than a revered intermediary. On offer is a mere promise of tranquillity and happiness. And at this point the philosophical schools agreed, believing that 'human beings are plunged in misery, anguish, and evil because they exist in ignorance'. Each school gave its pupils the following promise, that through its precepts they would be delivered from evil by learning to relate to the world differently. Hence the philosophers' advice: 'Evil is to be found not within things, but in the value judgements which people bring to bear *upon* things'.[45] The good offered by education could not be grasped in advance. The ignorant must assent to it before it arrives.

*

Before Socrates, educational subjectivities were simply defined. The itinerant Sophists, perhaps the first to distinguish themselves as educators, are credited with formalising education, transforming it from an activity involving 'non-specialized contact with the adult world' to an endeavour involving teachers working in an artificial environment. But the Sophists were attacked as mere 'salesmen of knowledge' investing little in the subjectivities of those they educated.[46] From Socrates onwards they were considered philosophically and morally inadequate. This established a judgemental hierarchy that survives to our present, where the most basic and disreputable mode of teaching approaches education as a mere process of 'putting in' or 'filling up'. Against this, Greek philosophy transformed education into a process of 'leading out' – the educator would now adopt the role of guide and exemplar, drawing out what is 'already there'. Purveyors of knowledge were replaced, or at least accompanied, by masters of the soul.

*

Philosopher educators were intimate on their own terms. With Socrates we observe how a philosopher-teacher might be bound to his pupils, often boys, through a 'loving' connection between master and disciple. This was billed as the first stage in the ascent of the master's soul. Through discipline and better control of the passions, the philosopher would begin to perceive in carnal love the poor reflection of its transcendent counterpart. This educational relationship established a model that more recent educational thinkers have sought to revive, much sanitised of course.[47] Their hope is to return depth and meaning to educational relationships that have become shallow and cynical. In their hands, intimacy stays with us as the saving grace of the educational good.

*

In an educational context intimacy ought not excite the body. Intimacy of an educational kind elevates the spirit. This is Plato's legacy, or the legacy of his kind of thinking. As Adriana Cavarero frames the problem, in her influential feminist critique: Plato's conception of philosophy may be intimate, but is hostile to life to the point of immaculate conception. Plato inaugurates in and of his philosophy the 'birth-giving male'. He conceives for ever more this educator of higher things.[48] Philosophy henceforth denigrates the physical procreation of birth-giving women. The mother who gives birth to life is superseded in thought by the philosopher who gives birth to ideas. According to this conceit, this fruit of masculine conception, there could be no higher calling than philosophy, of giving birth to ideas by one's own sex. Unlike women who produce in body nothing that endures beyond death, the philosopher (and misogynist) gives birth as he conceives: namely, in spirit.

*

Only well into modernity does the birth-giving teacher develop 'feminine' attributes, and this is associated with, but not reducible to, increased numbers of women employed as school teachers.[49] This transition occurs as boundaries between wage-labour and home life take form, as capital invests the latter, exploiting and conducting the unpaid labour of its female occupants. Education follows into the home, and into the kitchen.[50] But in schools and universities there is a parallel shift, as the caring teacher acquires gendered characteristics, and classed ones too.[51] She may be a mother, and as such, as teacher and mother, her emotional labour can be assumed, taken for granted and taken from her. The emotional labour of the educator becomes the irrefutable but unrewardable mainspring of education.

*

As women teachers exchanged the 'basic' teaching of the household or dame school for that of the more respectable teacher, we educators and educated people inherit with her the perspective of philosophy. The woman teacher acquires male characteristics, in the sense that she is expected to take forward an educational tradition that was profoundly masculine in conception, a tradition contrasting the pursuit of eternals to the distractions of having a body. Educators hereby remained wedded to intellectual creations designed to transcend or better manage the frailties of human existence. Aligned to that intellectual pretence, educators and educated people hoped to place themselves beyond scorn, the scorn of an educated class. With female attributes, they bore the burden of birth-giving men.[52]

The Cynical Educator

III

BENEVOLENT EDUCATORS

The Great Educational Swindle
On earth philosophy is remarkably accommodating, despite claims to be at one remove from worldly things. With the Greek philosophical schools in decline, practices were adapted to new contexts. Admittedly, in late antiquity the odd philosopher still gathered an audience, as willing spectators were educated in a revived Platonism, for instance.[1] Philosopher educators still existed in that sense, holding their own against the 'barbarian theosophy' of the early Christians.[2] But the Athenian schools had largely dissipated, their legacies co-opted to the educational demands of an aristocratic Roman elite. A smattering of Greek philosophy was now expected of those who considered themselves cultured. Conceptions of the educational good taken from classical antiquity, originally crafted for only a few disciples, were

passed to new contexts. They were passed on to a far more dispersed and diverse group of jobbing aristocrats more concerned with maintaining a cultivated air, than subordinating themselves to a specific philosophical order. In this context the Roman educator begins to operate rather differently. Attempts are still made to bind educator and pupil in a relationship where the educational good promised by the former is to be believed by the latter. Yet the educator more commonly took the position of private tutor or counsellor employed by a social superior, than revered head of a philosophical school.[3] This deepened the plight of an educational good to be followed but forever deferred.

*

The notion of philosopher as necessary eccentric (Socrates) or institutional head (a Plato, Epicurus, or Zeno) gradually gave way. Those providing spiritual direction no longer spoke from the security of a revered position or philosophical school. Educators increasingly offered counsel from positions directly subservient to power, being dependent upon their patrons for support. At its extreme, the educator combined his moral and spiritual superiority – his justification for employment – with servile gestures and near obsequious tact. Such hirelings were clearly not latter-day Sophists, winning customers by promising much and delivering little. At least they did not present themselves so. They continued to work within the tradition of ancient Greek philosophy that had long set itself against cheap imitators. Wisdom, for these Roman tutors represented more than a technique or body of knowledge that could be bought as and when convenient. It demanded lifelong commitment. But there was a shift nonetheless in the history of educational subjectivity. We have the makings of a social role in which the educator experiences great responsibility – the care of the soul no less – combined with a nagging sense of insecurity. The educator suffers the perpetual fear that one's masters will decide one's mastery is no longer required.

*

There is, in the Roman period, extensive discussion about the relationship between *parrhesia*, or speaking freely, and its antithesis which is flattery.[4] The problem is this: How to prevent the educator and social inferior from only telling his patron what he wishes to hear? How to build a relationship in which frank speech – necessary for reorienting the employer's soul – can be safely delivered? It would seem that the educator can only respond to this impossible situation by developing and strengthening the relationship which binds pupil to teacher. The teacher cannot rely upon reputation or respect alone, nor can the educator expect to hold the pupil's attention by force. It is necessary, in other words, to establish an educational tradition driven to convince its patrons of the benevolence if not dire necessity of their education before all else.

*

These fragments may sound distant, for we inhabit their echo. The great educational swindle of late antiquity reaches us, distorted. The educational good we inherit was first promoted from a position of weakness: the educator's weakness in the case of the hired teacher. It was the product of a servile relationship between educator and patron; an expression not merely of the need to convince, but a need to please. The Roman educator would justify himself to his employer, and say: 'Though the educational remedy on offer is worthwhile, it must bring discomfort.' True to the tradition of Greek philosophy, education will cause pain when it instructs those lacking in virtue, when it harries them to reorient their being. The educator must convince his patron that despite all the discomfort involved, education is worth the investment.

*

Hired teachers handled their employers with care, avoiding overly severe reprimands or regimes of instruction. In the education of his passions, an employer is advised to exercise only a 'gentle violence on the body'.[5] It was futile, these tutors counselled with undeniable cunning, to overrule the body in such a complete and tyrannical manner that it be injured by excessive denial and self-discipline. But a good measure of self-control was still advised. Patrons were told, and subsequently told one another,[6] that they would not govern others well if they could not first govern themselves. Rather conveniently, influential patrons were invited to apply the same principle of measure to the government of those beneath them, as they would to themselves. With care, education negotiates its field of violence.

*

As philosophy lost its old securities – that is, once pupils ceased flocking to the philosopher educator, once the philosopher educator increasingly becomes an educator philosopher, and finally, simply an educator – new means are found by which the educator binds himself to his pupils.[7] Writing in the second century, acting as personal physician to several Roman emperors,[8] Galen prepares a text that is educational in a dual sense. It both defines the role of educator and educates the tastes of those seeking to employ such an individual. In this book, *On the Passions and Errors of the Soul*, Galen explains how the powerful and rich are in need of honest educators, since most remain silent out of fear, or engage in flattery. As a consequence, those wishing to be educated well, must first make themselves weak:

> If, therefore, anyone who is either powerful or also rich wishes to become good and noble, he will first have to put aside his power and riches, especially in these times when he will not find a Diogenes who will tell the truth even to a rich man or a monarch.[9]

Galen gives his noble reader the following counsel: If, after several days, your guide has not reproached you for your passions, which must assuredly be clouding your reason, assume he has been negligent, that he is unwilling to help, or that 'he remains silent because he is afraid to reproach you'. It is for this last reason you must 'look upon him as your deliverer' and tell him so, making him promise from the outset to reveal your passions as if he were saving you 'from an illness of the body'.[10] There will be no recriminations, you must assure him. But if your guide still fails to reproach, employ another. To receive honest guidance become known as someone who endures, if not welcomes, unwelcome advice. You will be rewarded by the attentions of those who at last feel free to give 'true correction'. Insolence is another matter. In this case 'be steadfast', replying not with passion, but with the better argument.[11] But Galen repeats over and again his argument for the importance of the educator or guide to be held in esteem, indeed valued most, when his advice and guidance is displeasing. Even insolent educators are to be tolerated with restraint. Those wishing to be educated must realise, Galen claims, that their greatest foe is self-love which deludes them into believing there is nothing wrong with their soul: Only 'the wise man is free from fault', and such men hardly exist, which 'is why you hear the philosophers of old saying that to be wise is to become like God' – it is an impossibility.[12] Hence most people who aspire to an educated soul – one that overcomes 'diseases of the soul' including 'lust for power', 'love of glory' and 'greed', becoming temperate and tranquil[13] – urgently require the assistance of a guide and educator of the type Galen has in mind. This educator will be a kind of doctor, for these roles are not clearly distinguished. Care of soul and care of body intermingle, leading to intrusions that are both moral and medical. And so, in the medical and philosophical advice of Galen, and also Plutarch, even one's deportment during sex is to be carefully prescribed.[14] Clearly, this kind of educator must feel free to identify faults of the most intimate kind, where the pupil (his employer, even his emperor) believes none to exist.

*

The educator makes himself weak whilst insisting on the value of his presence. Despite his long training, exemplary self-discipline, temperance and tranquillity, his poise and achievements, the educator remains humble. Humility is one of his distinctions. He will 'look with scorn on glory', Galen explains, holding 'only the truth in esteem'. He will remain alert to those passions that might still claim him. He will not demand all acknowledge his excellence, though it has taken him a lifetime to cultivate. For 'the desire to have all men praise me is like the desire to possess all things', it is symptomatic of greed.[15] This educator will be content to remain unpopular at times, and even be a little resented. He will be generous and proceed as if all members of the aristocracy, however ravaged by 'diseases of the soul', can be redeemed.[16] It is in the educator's self-interest, after all, to forever work in the hope that all can be saved, that 'all the men with whom we spend our time' will come to share our own sensibilities, that with patience they will become like us. He nevertheless accepts his work will be limited by the self-love of those he teaches, and by variations in their nature, believing that: 'If their nature will accept the advantage of our care, they could become good men. If they should fail to accept this attention, the blame would not be ours'.[17] The educator will commit himself to unstinting effort, combining the poise of an educated man, the airs of a cultivated soul, and the humility of a noble servant who seduces his master with generosity of spirit.

*

With Seneca and Marcus Aurelius[18] we find the same recurring problem: how to justify the role of the educator, how to convince those in power of the necessity of the educator's intrusive advice. This educator self-consciously exhibits the best intentions. He exudes sincerity and devotion. By speaking freely at moments that are carefully chosen, the educator seeks to establish a bond with his pupil, declaring in effect: 'Look, I risk telling you the truth, so I must be on your side.'

*

The survival of an educational scheme involving delicately negotiated relations of power, where wealthy patrons are taught to welcome unwelcome advice, to lay themselves open to the scrutiny of those they employ, appears odd against the backdrop of an empire that was becoming 'frankly authoritarian'. These educational relations seem rather quaint, if not completely out of touch with the politics of a 'vast, despotic empire'.[19] In such a context there would, one presumes, be little patience for the cultured refinements of educated persons still cleaving to the role of 'disinterested advisor', to the figure of the philosopher-tutor. There would, one assumes, be little indulgence of the educated supplicant, who attempts to 'sway the will of the powerful' through intrusive practices that recommend discomfort and self-abasement. It seems odd at first sight that *paideia* (as this system of education and refinement is called), was still championed, bringing with it the expectation of 'a benevolent, because cultivated, exercise of authority', where all members of the upper class are said to benefit from common codes of courtesy and self-control. [20] Yet despotism over vast territories requires extended networks of support in order to function. Within these frameworks *paideia* thrived, greasing the wheels of imperial machinery by negotiating its violence. [21] More than this, *paideia* expressed the morality of an increasingly weakened aristocracy, living in a world 'characterized by a chilling absence of legal restraints on violence in the exercise of power'. A 'lurking fear of arbitrary violence', caused elites fearful of maintaining their position to fall back on the advantages of their educated refinement. [22] Educators could, then, appeal to a common fear of that 'tide of horror' which 'lapped close to the feet of all educated persons'[23] who were only exempt from corporal punishment because of their noble status. Educators could appeal to patrons who recognised the advantages of a culture of refinement in which anger is seen as a 'failure in decorum', and clemency is viewed as a manifestation of the dignity and poise of the powerful. [24] It was sufficiently obvious that ceremony and decorum 'did not simply exalt the powerful; it controlled them, by ritualizing their responses and bridling their raw nature through measured gestures'. [25] The noble ideal of character formation was then, a moral formation born of weakness, the weakness of a class of notables seeking to maintain its position. It assured that within the imperial system, cultured individuals or educated people were still treated as such. On occasion, favoured members of their class would even be permitted to speak back to the powerful, themselves now adopting the role of educated supplicants. This was the context within which the seductions of the educator-employee gained purchase. As Christianity subsequently took hold across the empire, these practices were not extinguished.

The philosopher educator was replaced by the Christian bishop, in the sense that the latter occupied the educational role established by the former, transforming this role, adapting its intrusions and seductions to new ends and contexts. This holy man would also at times offer unwelcome advice to his emperor, but with divine backing and the implied threat of God's wrath if left unheeded. Such bishops still practiced *paideia* then, though there had been an important shift: *Paideia* 'was no longer treated as the all-embracing and supreme ideal of a gentleman's life', rather it was viewed 'as the necessary first stage in the life cycle of the Christian public man'. It had been reduced in status, becoming mere preparatory schooling to a wider project of Christian character formation.[26]

A Christian Soul

For a time, Christianity existed as just another cult gaining influence as the Roman Empire degenerated.[27] The Roman elite, wanting philosophy for themselves, regarded with disgust that other great philosophical inheritance found across sects sweeping through Empire, with all their 'vagabonds, preachers, moralists, cults and communities'. They 'turned up their noses' at Christians as they did at the tattered, shameless Cynics.[28] Christianity would, of course, eventually triumph over its detractors. Not only did it assimilate itself to the ideology of the ruling order, it redefined and took over what it meant to be both cultured and educated. The other sects, including the Cynics, would only survive to the extent they were incorporated.

*

The Western 'soul' became the property of Christian theology, the 'educated soul' being itself Christianised.

This Christian appropriation took its time. A first century follower such as Paul the Apostle had little interest in the soul as distinct from the body, speaking in the latter case only of the 'flesh'. The flesh stood here for the general condition of humankind soon to be judged at the Second Coming of Christ. It was the plight of human beings caught in a 'hurried instant'.[29] But as Christ failed to materialise, first century Christians were forced to realise their collective sojourn on earth would be somewhat extended. It was now worth asking, as the ancients once had, how on earth the soul might protect itself from the impulses of the body. Here Christianity borrowed from its philosophical predecessors. And so, we encounter in Christian hands the following recognisably Stoic advice: 'Live as if you were going to die every day, devoting attention to yourselves and remembering my exhortations'.[30] Or the Platonic line: Approach your life as 'a training for death and a flight from the body' since the soul must be separated from the body if it is to know God.[31] Wisdom is reconceived as knowledge of God. It remains an otherworldly thing, approached only through death.

*

Where pagan philosophers educated their desires, Christians went much further: 'our ideal is not to experience desire at all', one said.[32] In principle, the egoistic self could be so undermined it would cease to desire completely, allowing the ascetic to arrive at a point where 'he has no will of his own'. This person would not 'want things to be as he wishes' since 'he wishes them to be as they are'.[33]

*

The body remained a training ground for the soul, furnishing it with all manner of edifying distractions. Ascetic practices such as fasting were hence designed to reconstitute the self so that body and soul would no longer be enslaved to the appetites.[34] Even illness was considered profitable by these Christian opportunists: 'You must consider your illness a pedagogue,' one said, 'which leads you to what is profitable to you – that is, teaches you to despise the body and corporeal things and all that flows away, is the source of worries, and is perishable, so that you may belong completely to the part which is above, ...making this life down below – as Plato says – a training for death... If you philosophize in this way, ...you will teach many people to philosophize in their suffering'.[35] The body may be loathsome, but was the best educational tool one had.[36]

*

Though Christian practices were geared to the formation of a spiritual elite, Christianity operated as a popular philosophy too. A Platonism for the masses, as Nietzsche put it.[37] Christianity cemented that educational commitment which holds all souls recoverable in principle. Until final judgement none are beyond redemption. And so, with Christianity, that 'flight from the body' inaugurated by Hellenistic philosophy persists and spreads. Strategies are developed and extended that control the appetites, restrain the passions, and thereby educate the soul.[38] Christianity continues to pursue objectives remaining beyond reach by definition. Down below in this life that persists despite everything it is taught to abhor about itself, the message is clear: You can aspire to a virtuous life despite all your bodily distractions, despite your debased existence. In pursuing virtue you will begin to approach knowledge of God. So go forth, be virtuous, but remember the path is difficult. In contemporary terms the formula is adjusted: Seek tranquillity in your classroom, cry out for a state of calm, cultivate a moment of interrupted calamity, make that your primary objective and sustain yourself by it. What else is there to hope for on earth?

*

Baptism offers an early example of Christian education. It involved a death of sorts, imitating the death and resurrection of Christ.[39] Baptismal preparation was an 'enterprise in mortification' by which those hoping to be baptised demonstrated the extent they were willing to die voluntarily, ending their earlier, sinful life through a final act of devotion.[40] These baptismal rituals demanded rigorous preparation and commitment, obeying the precept: 'no baptism without prior teaching'.[41] To be purified the soul would have to be first educated, or formed. Exercises such as fasting and sexual abstinence ensued. These obeyed a demonology whereby spirits unable to enjoy bodily pleasures directly, are forced to enjoy them vicariously through their human host. These spirits are most active when the body is moved by those pleasures they seek to share.[42] Hence, the quest for Christian spiritual purity is associated with a fight to limit pleasurable activities. The early Christian begins to observe life-denial as an ongoing problem. Such denials precede but reach beyond baptism, giving us the roots of a practice that would extend to occupy the entire life – a life of denials – of the practicing Christian.

*

There was some disagreement concerning when, at which point exactly, baptismal purification occurred. Was it during immersion, or was purification a prerequisite for baptism? In the former case, baptism in water was analogous to baptism in blood, namely, martyrdom. Unlike martyrdom, water baptism was complicated by the ongoing life of the baptised. The baptised soul would remain attached to the body after the event. In this case, rather a lot – perhaps too much – was expected of the ritual. Hence a whole machinery of self-purification prior to baptism was developed. The baptised would not only believe in the moment of baptism through an act of faith. They would commit to the educational process that preceded it. Hence the canonical statement: 'We are not bathed in the baptismal water in order to be purified, but we are bathed in the baptismal water because we are purified'.[43] For this education to be a success, it was necessary to convince the soon-to-be baptised it was worthy of commitment. And so in a different context, serving a different purpose, a familiar problem recurs: how to convince the educatee of the educational good. In the second and third centuries the Christian solution differs from its pagan cousins. It gives care of soul over to the pupil. The pupil rather than the tutor now operates as guarantor to the educational good. The educator remains, yet becomes more of an educational conduit than a self-possessed guide. When things go awry, the educator can claim: 'You have nobody to blame but yourself.' The obsequious plea of the Roman tutor is replaced by the knowing look of the baptismal teacher.

*

Catechumens – candidates for baptism – were presented to the teachers by their sponsors. During this initial examination the candidate's intentions and prior life were put to the test.[44] A number of professions were prohibited, including brothel keepers, prostitutes, unfaithful concubines, men who kept concubines, pagan teachers, magicians, astrologers, pagan priests, gladiators, soldiers and charioteers.[45] If admitted, catechumens embarked on a training period of some months or years, concluding with another examination testing how piously they lived since joining. Those considered ready underwent more intense preparation, involving ascetic practices (such as prayer, fasting, kneeling) that were, through their rigor, 'intended to test the authenticity of the faith'.[46] Two days before baptism, the catechumen underwent exorcism carried out by the bishop. As the bishop uttered imprecations to drive out Satan, the catechumen was expected to listen 'without moving or fidgeting' thereby proving 'the spirit of evil is no longer master of his soul'.[47] Those who became agitated, perhaps foaming at the mouth, gnashing their teeth, or becoming excessively uplifted, would be placed to one side for further cleansing.[48] Exorcism was not simply about purging the soul in final preparation for baptism; it was a procedure by which those to be purified were expected to manifest the truth they were ready for baptism.[49] Clearly there was a voluntary dimension to baptismal initiation, where it was believed 'lack of success in expelling the alien spirits was due to the candidate's failure to receive his instructions in good faith'.[50] 'Uncleanness' at this late juncture was considered the catechumen's fault, since the devil could not have survived this far without assistance.[51] In Augustine's words:

> We heap upon you the curses that his wickedness deserves; but you on your side declare a most glorious war against him by your aversion and your pious renunciation... This is now your task, this is your labour.[52]

During baptism a last test was applied. At this point, so it was hoped, the Holy Spirit would descend into the soul of the baptised. Three questions were asked: Do you believe in the Father? Do you believe in the Son? Do you believe in the Holy Spirit? The baptised would reply to each, and be submerged three times.[53] Yet the ceremonies continue: 'And when he has done exorcising, let him [the bishop] breathe in their face. And when he has sealed their foreheads and their ears and their noses, let him raise them up. And let them spend all the night in vigil, and let them be read to and instructed'.[54] The devil, one presumes, was still present, 'fighting for control of his victims' who, once cleansed, had to be safeguarded against re-entry.[55] The candidate for baptism had been tested repeatedly and with increased severity, right until the moment of purification. Educationally, everything that could be done had been done to assure success. Procedures had been instituted, attention had been lavished. At each stage a concerned gaze was fixed on the soul of the candidate, raising the stakes of failure, further intensifying pressure on the baptised to demonstrate success.

*

The levels of purification achieved through baptism were always limited. Christianity insisted all members of its congregation would 'remain a little impure', at least in this life.[56] Hence, the work of redemption was never-ending. Tranquillity would be desired, and fervently pursued, but never entirely achieved. Here the Christian soul differs from Greek antiquity by the addition of original sin.[57] A specifically Christian conception of human frailty and its overcoming takes form, where nobody, however pure, has the necessary strength to step outside convention and remain faithful to God. All must submit to the protection of the Church. Unlike the Platonic soul which loses its knowledge of higher things, or the soul of the neo-Platonists which 'falls into matter'[58] becoming 'harmed and diminished by association'[59] – the Christian soul is gradually understood according to the fall of Adam. This soul is still troubled by the body, and the hope remains it will be liberated when the latter passes on. But the Christian soul is not so much educated through a (Platonic) process of ascent and rediscovery by which it aspires to wisdom (and death). Rather, it is formed through a constant battle with the evil it contains. The risk, clearly enough, is that its demons will follow to the afterlife, which means that the educational drama of redemption is no longer one of 'progressive illumination', but one of struggle and perpetual suspicion. [60] Reconceived as knowledge of God, wisdom is similarly transformed, becoming ever more desired, yet ever more remote and unachievable. Nobody is rescued by force of will alone from a fallen condition, since 'every act of will is infected by the very condition from which it needs to be rescued'. Success is reliant upon God's grace, committing each Christian subject to an educational project that remains, by definition, 'incomplete in this present life'.[61] The Christian cultivates spiritual success as an obsessional objective, in a context where only failure manifests.

*

A transformed, evil Satan lies behind the coming educational drama of early Christianity. In the Testaments Satan was not yet evil personified. He was custodian on earth, a mere 'functionary' of divine government 'charged with testing and disciplining Mankind'.[62] Satan first takes form as examiner, testing the faith of God's people. The fall of Satan only occurred as Christianity evolved in late antiquity, with Satan becoming God's adversary instead, the personification of radical evil. In educational terms, the greatest external examiner ever imagined was hurled from his office. Since their examiner on earth had departed, Christians were forced to examine themselves, fearing that if they failed to do so adequately Satan would return and take up residence within. For fear of Satan, the educational mission of Christianity became inescapable, since the 'more Christian one is, the more one is at risk...the more the devil rages' against his expulsion from the soul.[63] The more Christian one became, the more one needed education.

*

Baptised Christians could still fall from grace. Centuries before the sale of indulgences became commonplace, fallen Christians would find salvation, if at all, only through a second penance, begging for admission once more to an educational order that makes shame and supplication a lifelong experience. Commitment to the educational good was again a condition of entry, this time to the 'order of penitents'.[64] Clearly the Christian was never safe and must never relax: the danger of sin 'never subsides'.[65] This introduced a new kind of fear, 'a sense of fear about oneself, of what one is'. This fear was more radical in its reach and constantly present than a 'fear of destiny' or of God's wrath.[66] It was the fear we might fail at any moment in our attempts to become free of Satan's grip. Thus motivated one toils ceaselessly until the moment of final deliverance... It would appear that a whole subjectivity, and a whole educational tradition, was built upon this fear of self. Education dealt again in conceptions of weakness, in this case, the inevitable weakness of the sinner who fears for his soul. Education recommended itself as the unflagging response, the first and last hope, against evil.

Sin Multiplied

Education swallows everything and anything, given the chance. Having become lost in its digestive tract, educational practitioners experience their confinement as if it were a stable condition, not realising they have been taken in and will eventually pass out. Its historians are similarly afflicted, most settled when locating their object within more immediate institutional confines. From this position, early Christian baptismal practices are not particularly educational, or hardly appear central to a history of education: 'If we must draw from our early Christian precursors, why not base our understanding in Christian monasticism, or the first Christian schools?' Or so resounds that tendency, which would have us confine education to its most obvious ancestral manifestations, strengthening an educated conceit that finds security in solidity. The Cynic replies with aperient measures, but cannot resist doubling back and probing its strongholds.

*

The first monks were uncultured, lowly and contemptible. Uneducated, they lacked *paideia*. The grubby ascetic was only later transformed,[67] eventually becoming the disciplined vanguard of a new elite, specialising in spiritual warfare. Here the occasional violence of fourth century monastic vigilantes, ransacking towns for idols, tearing down synagogues and pagan shrines, coalescing as lynch mobs,[68] only reflected those more sustained, far more constantly exerted inner aggressions by which monks disciplined themselves in acts of pious devotion. These monks were 'warriors of the spirit',[69] and described themselves in such militant terms.[70] But it was not all violence, or at least, some violence was benign in appearance. These monastic orders not only preyed through acts of terror, but installed themselves as distributors of welfare to those they persecuted.[71] In a similar way, the violence of monastic self-discipline was matched by its claim to be the most benignant of exertions ever made upon the human soul. To erase the presence of sin and save the soul, monasticism recommended itself.

*

Within the walls of the monastic institution, another interiority was constructed. Those seeking redemption were no longer asked simply to exhibit themselves as fallen beings. There was an expectation to divide and inspect one's being, multiplying its potential for sin. This newfound depth was cosmic, rather than personal, since the details of a monk's inner life were expressive of exterior forces. Hence sexual renunciation was not a matter of treating one's individual desires, proclivities and so on, as if they were 'lodged in the isolated body'. Rather, the task facing the monk and early Christian 'drew its seriousness' from the cosmic scale of the battle, where those energies pulsing through the body were 'the same energies that kept the stars alive'.[72] Individual privacy had little meaning in this context. Sex was just another bodily distraction 'overshadowed by the most obscene disruption of all in the texture of the universe' – 'the parting of the body and soul at death'. Sexual renunciation or at least discipline was only valuable in giving a 'manageable face to the diffuse horror of mortality'. It provided an outlet where early Christians could gain some measure of control. By denying those forces that were expressive of life, of its drive for continuity through reproduction, early Christians believed themselves able to 'install a place in the human heart where the footsteps of death might be muffled'.[73] The point was to pre-empt death by practicing mortifications of one's own. This made sense because life itself had little intrinsic value. Earthly existence was considered the 'product of an over-riding demonic tyranny'[74] whose end Christ inaugurated. It was the duty of each Christian to hasten the collapse of that tyranny by refusing to satisfy sexual desires.[75] Other justifications soon followed. For Origen (pious to the point of self-castration) earthly pleasures were considered mere 'slurred echoes' of those heavenly delights reserved for the pious.[76] In the monastery, practices designed to attack these existential slurs became highly developed.

Whilst baptism, and then penance, sought to rescue the soul from its fallen state, monasticism refined the soul it rescued. It turned attention to those recesses where sin might hide. Monasticism still implied a life of penance, yet penance was now tied to the production of sin. The monk would cultivate his soul through a mortification of the flesh far more diligent and persevering.

*

Traceable to the third century if not earlier, Christian monasticism was a way of life for the social outcast. Early monks lived alone or in groups, either in the desert or on the fringe of society. The subsequent history of monasticism is the history of their institutionalisation, of the social outcast who becomes socially useful. Aspiring monks no longer walked into the desert. They stood at the monastery gate. According to Cassian, they waited for days as monks within heaped abuse on those seeking admission. Only having endured such humiliations would they be admitted, exchanging their clothes for the habit of the order, renouncing all prior wealth, becoming entirely dependent. The second admission might take a year, during which the candidate was permitted to live on the outskirts of the monastery performing menial tasks. Following tests of patience, obedience, submission and humility, the candidate might finally be allowed to join the order.[77] An indefinite period followed during which the novice would be taught to further renounce his will. Any wishes or inclinations that contradicted his orders, even if they were never realised, were to be confessed to an elder. Each monk was expected to 'obey in everything and to hide nothing', to 'obey exhaustively and exhaustively tell what one is'.[78]

*

Monastic institutions were not reliant on the greatness of their teachers or spiritual leaders. They would not transfer wisdom downwards. The monastic life was still a philosophical life in the ancient sense, reorienting the soul whilst deferring wisdom. And yet, monasteries no longer required the guidance of a 'great philosopher' in order to function.[79] This was a sensible precaution given their susceptibility to temptation and sin. Even great monks and spiritual leaders could fall from grace. And so, in the monastic orders envisaged by Cassian, and later by Benedict,[80] the 'corporate body of the monastery' rather than the piety of any single leader, 'bridles the dangerous assertion of the individual will and its accompanying cravings'.[81] Obedience remained absolutely necessary to monastic life, yet students were not obedient because of the greatness of the teacher who knew better; rather, they were obedient for the sake of obedience, remaining obedient even when the teacher was no longer worthy of it. Elders and teachers were not given licence to fail their students; they too would be subject to the strictures of monastic life. Yet, the monastic institution did not depend upon their excellence for its survival. Such teachers did not yet carry the success of education, and the educational encounter, on their conscience.

*

Monastic obedience was not demanded to render education more efficient. An efficient transfer of knowledge, or wisdom, from master to student was not its object. Monastic obedience did not derive its authority from the 'quality of the order' nor was it reliant on the 'quality of the person' giving the order.[82] The fact the student obeyed, whatever the order, was more important. Cassian reports a whole number of absurd orders and requests to make this point, that obedience is the basic condition of monastic life.[83] The monk 'obeys in order to be obedient'[84] ideally reaching a state of obedience so absolute he is ready to obey even before he receives the order. When orders are wanting, the monk must see to it that events take on 'the form and value of an order'. The monk fills his world with orders, experiencing everything as an order, so there is 'no act in the monk's life that is not a response to an order or, at the least, a reaction to permission given'. [85] In part the monk experiences everything as an order because he is expected to place himself 'as low as possible in relation to everyone else'. Believing himself to be a sinner, he must 'consider himself more humble than any of his companions' accepting their wishes as if they were commands.[86] His extreme humility, giving himself over to the will of others, prepares the monk to cease willing entirely. The aim of obedience, thus understood, is the eventual 'mortification of one's will; it is to act so that one's will, as one's own will, is dead'.[87] And so, whilst monasteries might be celebrated in the popular imagination for their great endurance, surviving the upheavals of history so they could preserve and pass on culture to future generations; their early philosophical outlook and educational ethos was one of extreme submission and deathly inertia.

*

Self-discipline should remain measured and sedate. Any self-denying ordinance pushed to excess risks becoming self-destructive. The monk risks succumbing to hubris. Cassian recalls monks casting themselves down wells, fasting excessively, or crossing deserts without food to demonstrate just how catastrophically they had purged themselves of natural inclinations and desires.[88] Despite appearances, these were not acts of extreme piety. They were symptomatic of a desire for glory, or so runs this line of critique. The monasteries of the fourth century were perhaps themselves established in response to the 'untrammelled intensification' of such practices. Some ascetic practitioners were becoming dangerously indifferent to pain and discomfort, removing themselves beyond the grasp of power.[89] In its advanced form asceticism posed a challenge to Christianity, delivering its practitioners beyond the influence of its institutions and teachings. The most potent ascetics effectively reversed the self-denials of monastic obedience, transforming these denials into a form of 'egoistic self-mastery' that denied access to external power.[90]

*

To secure their foothold monastic and ecclesiastical institutions had to bring self-mastery back within their control. They would purge themselves of all vagrant, self-sufficient, ascetic heresies, and bring all miracles, marvels, punishments and self-flagellations back into the orbit of their influence. This was achieved in part by the idea that the devil present within us cannot be cast out alone. He may lie concealed behind those acts we consider most holy. Excessive fasting, for example, could be the devil's work, as he weakens those abstaining from food so they cannot resist other temptations. Hence the monk learns to exercise discrimination, moderating his devotional activities where necessary, inspecting every inclination and thought. Such processes of inspection (seeking to cast out the devil's trickery, including illusions of piety implanted by the devil) were to be carried out under the auspices of an institutional framework, where one monk relies upon the ear of another. This ear must not become too friendly, however. In some early monasteries young monks were expected 'to maintain a distance of one cubit between each other's bodies'.[91] The monk to whom one confesses does not have to be an intimate, nor does this monk require greater powers of discrimination. As Foucault suggests in his critique of confessional practices; the monk to whom one confesses is merely an instrument in the moral architecture of the monastery, where the purpose of confession is not so much to appeal to another's better judgement. The form of confession is more important than the wisdom of the person to whom one speaks; 'the quality of the person to whom one speaks, the advice he might be able to give, and his experience' is less important than 'the simple fact of speaking'. The main feature of confession is not the authority of the master, but the fact one confesses 'to someone who is basically an x'.[92] Confession expresses and brings to the surface thoughts and feelings, however fleeting, that each monk may have otherwise ignored or been able to forget. Their 'objective content', whether they are true or false, is less important than what they reveal about the preoccupations of the thinker.[93] These thoughts are to be sifted through. They are symptomatic of the soul that is given form and made available to inspection through confession. The expectation is that confession becomes perpetual and continuous, allowing the 'flow of thoughts that ceaselessly agitate the monk's soul' to be put under constant supervision.[94] This obligation to confess ties the monk to his community, forcing him to establish a connection where submission is accompanied by a great deal of disclosure. The monk not only gives up his freedom and renounces his will, he commits to making himself known, permanently and in almost every detail, so that he can be acted upon. This is designed to turn the monk's inner world 'inside out' leaving nothing remaining that could not be placed before others.[95] There would be nothing left that could be privately willed. At its best and most effective, evil forces are no longer feared because they are concealed, they are not found lurking behind a façade of faithful devotion. Rather, the monastery produces its evil tidings, it multiplies sin through relentless confessional practices, as compulsive as they are conditional.

*

In monastic communities it was considered a privilege to visit good Christian violence upon oneself – mortifying the flesh, engaging in self-denial, submitting to endless inspection – for only those willing to prostate themselves before the gates of the community were admitted and trained to do so. This began that process by which members renounced their will, so as to approach an educational good that would never be realised, regardless of the devotions of an entire community working its regimen. It would never be manifested, either in pious individuals or pious acts, for these individuals and their actions would always be suspected for their vainglory. Whenever the educational good becomes manifest, it is to be doubted as the devil's work. The educational good functions as its own aperient.

*

In a pre-modern context, the educational good is postponed yet affirmed. It seduces but never delivers. It is as fervently believed as it is cloaked, operating a system that ties its pursuers to an educational path along which hope is forced but never realised. It ensnares the educated and those about to be educated. It attaches its victims to an educational promise that remains forever empty. It conjures the educated soul and bases its conceit in processes of self-doubt and suspicion. It is born of weakness, reinforcing the weakness of those who educate and weakening those educated by them. It inaugurates a line of descent where nothing suffices but everything must be done. We must always fall short and remain within its shadow.

IV

OUR EDUCATIONAL CONSCIENCE

The Healthy Educator
The philosopher educator becomes educator philosopher. And then, finally, educator without philosophy. This is the history of Western education.

*

Seneca anticipated the second coming of educator philosopher in the first century, offering the following counsel:

> Avoid shabby attire, long hair, an unkempt beard…and all other misguided means to self-advertisement. The very name of philosophy, however modest the manner in which it is pursued, is unpopular enough as it is: imagine what the reaction would be if we started dissociating ourselves from the conventions of society. Inwardly everything should be different but our outward face should conform to the crowd… Let our aim be a way of life not

diametrically opposed to, but better than that of the mob. Otherwise we shall repel and alienate the very people whose reform we desire.[1]

The philosopher's life must be 'a compromise between the ideal and the popular morality. People should admire our way of life but they should at the same time find it understandable'.[2] The philosopher must not appear too otherworldly. A Stoic may wish to live in conformity with nature, but should not torture his body, 'make a point of being dirty' or 'adopt a diet that is not just plain but hideous and revolting... Philosophy calls for simple living, not for doing penance'.[3] The art of seduction depends upon a respectable appearance. The educator philosopher accommodates himself to his contemporaries.

*

Whilst the Stoic philosopher prepares himself each day to endure any possible misfortune, he should not seek it out. He will enjoy whatever he is able to accumulate. Only fools and those of unstable mind find wealth to be an 'intolerable burden'.[4] The secret, Seneca decides, is to avoid becoming overly attached to material things; prepared to give them up if forced. Even friendships are to be enjoyed without becoming dependent upon them.[5] Here the relationship between tutor and patron may be modelled on friendship, but the tutor must not invest himself in the success of his pupil. In his musings *On the Shortness of Life,* Seneca laments, most squander their lives servicing the needs of others, paying too little attention to their own: 'Think how much of your time was taken from you by a creditor, how much by a mistress, how much by a patron, how much by a client.'[6] Attending to others may bring benefits, even fame and glory, but these attendant folk will have hardly lived, busying themselves as they 'scurry to and fro', spreading themselves too thin.[7] Under these conditions 'no one is his own person' having wasted energies on others.[8] When they eventually 'come to face death', these 'wretches' are already destroyed. For they busied themselves too long 'in doing nothing'.[9] Unlike the philosopher they discover too late that a life spread thin is a life wasted. They beg for just a little more time of their own before they depart. By contrast the philosopher stares death in the face knowing his life was well spent. The dying philosopher consoles himself that he lived in contemplation of higher things. His life was a cultivation of self. The philosopher of this more ancient tradition has not squandered his life. He was not distracted by useless diversions, having realised long ago that before all else he must attend to his own being, using all the time he is given to master his existence and make of it something worthwhile. For the Stoic, self-mastery is also a form of self-sufficiency, where Seneca has in mind a rather heroic yet leisured figure. His soul being raised so high, his self-mastery being so well practised, this figure 'carries his valuables intact through cities burnt to ashes'.[10] As an educator, and as a philosopher, the Stoic hopes to become impregnable. He remains true to himself, true to his philosophy, a generous benefactor to humankind.

*

The educated conceit of the Stoic philosopher was somewhat muddied under Christian influence. Christianity intensified that process of introspection by which the philosopher endlessly toils towards a form of self-perfection never to be realised, only approximated. The educator must now carry intact not only his valuables, but the valuables of those he teaches through cities burnt to ashes. The plight of the educator's soul becomes fettered to the plight of those to be educated. Eventually such teachers would carry the success of education, and the educational encounter, on their conscience.

*

Seneca gave intimate advice but lacked an educational conscience. His advice was that of the doctor who attends to your health yet remains distant. Since his good-health remains unaffected by your ill-health, the educator's health is secure regardless of whether or not you ignore his advice, or fail to take his prescriptions. Your fate is not tied to his own.

*

'Without wisdom,' Seneca writes to his pupil, 'the mind is sick, and the body itself, however physically powerful, can only have the kind of strength that is found in persons of demented or delirious state'.[11] It is 'silly' and 'no way for an educated man to behave, to spend one's time exercising the biceps, broadening the neck and shoulders and developing the lungs. Even when extra feeding has produced gratifying results and you've put on a lot of muscle, you'll never match the strength or the weight of a prize ox'. The educated man, must 'make room for the spirit', keeping the body within more reasonable bounds.[12]

*

Recalling that convention by which letters are begun, 'I trust this finds you as it leaves me, in good health', Seneca prefers the following salutation: 'I trust this finds you in pursuit of wisdom'.[13] Crucially, the recipient is to be assured his tutor and advisor is already well on the way. The Roman tutor is employed because of his independent refinements. He sets himself against all false educators who teach 'how to argue instead of how to live'.[14] The liberal arts in general come under attack by Seneca, insofar as they lead in that direction.[15] We must reject those who offer lessons that have little bearing on the way they live. 'People prone to every fault they denounce, are walking advertisements to the uselessness of their training'.[16] The educator philosopher teaches by example, though he does so without alienating the very people whose reform he desires. Exemplary though he may be, the educator remains cautious and alert. He bears the employer in mind.

*

'I, Seneca, am worthy of employment precisely because I bear out my lessons in my actions.' It is the philosopher's self-mastery that qualifies him for favourable employment, and not his favourable employment that guarantees his self-worth. But under the yoke of medieval Christianity, a reversal occurs. The work of the educator, the educator's achievements rather than the educator's independent refinements, increasingly provide succour in a context of rising insecurity. Indeed the self-worth of the educator is rendered precarious by a growing attachment, Seneca might say over-attachment, to the plight of those to be educated. The conceit of the educator is no longer guaranteed independently of education. It must be secured through education. The educator can no longer rely upon his status as philosopher. His conceit now depends on his status as educator. The self-reinforcing esteem of the philosopher who lives the exemplary life, who represents the epitome of philosophical excellence, is replaced, whereupon the esteem of the educator, if not the educator's soul, is dependent on the educator's good work.

Principles of Pastoral Care

We owe much to the Christian pastorate. Its logic of power comes to define the subjectivity of the Western educator. It binds the educator to his pupils by committing the educator to a project of mutual redemption. Of pre-Christian and Hebraic conception, it continues even now to provide the 'core moral technology of the school'. For its principles of care were not reducible to theological propositions. They would 'eventually slip their doctrinal moorings' and 'quietly migrate' to a secular context.[17]

*

In its early forms pastoral power held within view not a territory, but a flock. Its deity the Hebrew God moves from place to place. His presence, as Foucault argues, 'is never more intense and visible than when his people are on the move' for in their wanderings they require direction.[18] Pastoral power offers guidance through uncertain terrain. Fundamentally 'a beneficent power', the shepherd-God operates a regime of power that exists in explicit contrast to those characterised by wealth, splendour and above all by their 'ability to triumph over enemies, defeat them, and reduce them to slavery'. The pastoral ruler, like the pastoral teacher, stands in contrast to regimes of force that may at times be beneficent too, but are not primarily so. Pastoral power is 'entirely defined by its beneficence; its only *raison d'être* is doing good'.[19] The shepherd desires the salvation of his flock. He guides it to good pasture; he cares for his flock as a whole and individually, retrieving strays.

*

Pastoral power is not allergic to displays of strength and superiority. But these are its occasional forms. The shepherd exerts a form of power less spectacular as it is more committed. The shepherd's power is notable for its 'zeal, devotion and endless application'.[20] To be a shepherd is not an honour, it is a burden. The shepherd directs all care and attention to others and rarely to himself. The good shepherd is selfless, serving as 'intermediary between the flock and pasture, food, and salvation'.[21] But the shepherd is also torn. He directs the flock as a whole, whilst ensuring no individual escapes his attention. He keeps 'an eye on all and on each'.[22]

*

The shepherd deals with impossible scenarios. Will he 'neglect the whole of the flock in order to save a single sheep?'[23] Or will he neglect a single sheep to save the flock? This theme is endlessly repeated 'from Genesis up to the rabbinical commentaries'[24] and becomes, in turn, the problem of the Church. Will it abandon, exclude or chase away the sheep that is a 'cause of scandal, or whose corruption is in danger of corrupting the whole flock'? Because here is the paradox of pastoral care: The flock's salvation depends upon the supervision of each sheep. The basic problem the Church faces again and again is to ask itself: What is to be done about those who stray, those who renounce the Church? A serious matter, for 'at the end of the day, at the end of life in the world' the Christian shepherd and pastor will 'have to account for every sheep'.[25] Any missing sheep, or sheep led astray, could be counted against him. The shepherd is forever answerable.

*

The pastor identifies with his congregation. He feels their pain and suffering as if it were his own. He carries every act of those in his care, every merit and fault. When good deeds are done, the pastor shares in them as if they were his own. Where evil surfaces, the pastor cannot help wondering if it were somehow his doing, from inattention at least, if not from false teaching.

*

The shepherd is prepared to die to save his sheep. He risks his soul for the souls of others. He becomes their confidant as he tells his flock to unburden their minds of every sin and indiscretion. Through confession he absolves those in his care, hearing their darkest thoughts, risking his own. Together they develop a conscience. By encountering such 'beautiful sinners', hearing their temptations to evil, he risks temptation himself. The pastor gambles so much but remains hopeful.[26] He believes himself saved by his commitment to die on their behalf. In this sacrifice lies his salvation – his last hope. But the hope which motivates his actions is of a kind never to be realised on earth. The pastor's salvation is in God's hands. He must remain uncertain of his success amid so much failure. His salvation, and theirs, is not guaranteed. It is never assured.

*

The pastor must recognise his imperfections and reveal a select few to his congregation. He must repent openly and show humility before his faults in 'a self-abasement that will edify the faithful'.[27] The conceit of the pastor – by which he justifies his elevated position as director of souls – is a product of his self-abasement. The pastor is not simply elevated. He is elevated by virtue of the fact that he, more than any other, recognises his fallen state, his incompleteness. The most conceited educator, by extension, is that educator who openly declares his incompleteness before his congregated pupils. Our most conceited educator of this tradition makes this proclamation, this declaration of his indefinite limitations the basis of his practice. He claims that only in this classroom, in communion with these pupils does he become what he must be. Only here, in this moment does he become an educator.

*

As an educational problem, the paradoxical equivalence of all sheep generates a dilemma that remains with us to this day. The care of all and each, the holding to account of educator to his actions as viewed through the lens of his pupils, the assumption that he will if necessary be their sacrificial victim, haunts education still. For the shepherd and educator whose *raison d'être* is to guide and protect, whose salvation depends on the success of his good work, this paradox becomes a source of considerable unsettlement.

*

Against those who mount the pulpit and those who congregate below. Against those who operate outside the Christian church adopting its techniques as their own, the following is due: Each gathering flock be warned. Each educational congregation take heed. Christianity 'coagulated all these themes of pastoral power into precise mechanisms and definite institutions'. It 'implanted its apparatuses within the Roman Empire' and organised at its heart a type of power perhaps 'unknown to any other civilization... Of all civilizations,' Foucault continues, 'the Christian West has undoubtedly been at the same time, the most creative, the most conquering, the most arrogant, and doubtless the most bloody'. Yet 'over millennia Western man has learned to see himself as a sheep in a flock, something that assuredly no Greek would have been prepared to accept. Over millennia he has learned to ask for his salvation from a shepherd'. This 'strangest form of power' one that 'is most typical of the West, and that will also have the greatest and most durable fortune...was born, or at least took its model from the fold, from politics seen as a matter of the sheep-fold'.[28]

*

The sceptic may agree; it is conceivable that a caring educator of conventional moral bearing might today still institute some principles of pastoral care. But surely most educators escape this scheme? They moralise, if at all, within a more permissive, liberal framework of influence. Radical educators in particular, who seek out power and intrigue everywhere, would surely be allergic to such morally managed relationships? Not necessarily. Though conventional moralities may have been replaced, pastoral care remains, indeed proliferates in those secular contexts where it is at the same time disavowed. Traditional flaws, those foibles we inherit from the pulpit, have been sociologically deepened. As such they still require careful, supervised extraction. Radical educators actually multiply our potential to err. They achieve this effect 'with an oppositional reading of the current stage of world history' and a reading of our unwitting participation in those systems that reproduce power and co-opt us as its agents. Exercises in pastoral care that involve self-examination and sustained introspection, are transformed to meet a new set of demands. The radical educator finds in each student not merely 'signs of conscience' but also 'symptoms of the relative ravages of patriarchy and capitalism' or whatever else fits the bill.[29] The radical educator negotiates such symptoms with care, cultivating an environment in which they may be expressed, 'owned' and willingly worked upon. The educator remains in place as our necessary though self-effacing guide. By thanks to this 'foremost virtuoso of conscience', we, along with education are to be redeemed.[30]

Educational Ill-Health

The shepherd-flock metaphor of 'care' should not be misunderstood as if it were a commitment to health. A priestly class and its descendant educators have common interest in making those in their care ill. In Nietzschean terms: The Christian and, by extension, educational pastorate has a 'life-interest in making mankind sick'[31] – where *making* sick is the true hidden objective of the Church's whole system of salvation procedures'.[32]

*

Making sick should not be understood in the form of an attack or infection. The pastorate does not inflict sickness upon its congregation, at least not at first. It begins by appealing to a sickness already present. Hence the Nietzschean line: 'No one is free to become a Christian or not to do so; one is not 'converted' to Christianity – one must be sufficiently sick for it'. That is, one must be predisposed to the sickness it cultivates.[33]

*

Continuities abound. The priest's interest is coterminous with the professional interest of the Roman educator, who must first convince his patron of the sickness of his soul. What changes nonetheless is the treatment. There is a shift in the realm of spiritual direction: Sickness once taught self-mastery, recommending submission to a philosophical regimen. With Christianity it breeds submission to a pastoral regime. In Antiquity spiritual direction was somewhat voluntary, where 'the person who wishes to be directed finds someone whom he asks to direct him'. Spiritual direction was also often paid for, as a consultation. This consultation was circumstantial; one's spiritual director would not take care of one's entire life.[34] Indeed, the educational objective was that the pupil would 'take control and become master of himself'.[35] By contrast, Christian spiritual direction is not oriented as with the ancients to self-mastery. Or at least, Christian self-mastery is now encouraged only to the extent it becomes 'an instrument of subordination'.[36] One does not consent to spiritual direction as one consents to palmistry. Submission was not voluntary in this sense, nor was it circumstantial. It relied upon a form of renunciation that was intended to become absolutely permanent. The purpose of spiritual direction was to develop a form of introspection that would 'fix more firmly the relationship of subordination'. It would attach its recipients to a regime of power that would take care of their entire life, in all its detail, and for the rest of its duration.[37]

*

Sickness becomes permanent; an irreparable disease; a perpetual disorder. Any hope of rescue demands obedience to a higher ordinance of salvation. From now on if mastery has any meaning, it means our enslavement. Though Christian self-denial was continuous with the ancient pursuit of mastery, it would push that ancient pursuit even further towards its self-denying conclusion. Christian denial is premised, as Nietzsche put it, on the idea that the "perfect soul' could be carried about in a cadaver of the body'.[38] To 'make himself *perfect* man was advised to draw his senses back into himself in the manner of the tortoise, to cease to have any traffic with the earthly, to lay aside his mortal frame.' Following which, so it was promised, 'the chief part of him would remain behind' as 'pure spirit'.[39] But pure spirit becomes 'pure stupidity' once we deduct its nervous system, its senses, its appetites.[40] Pure stupidity is the sickness Western education would have us suffer. Few attain it. My own stupidity is only the larger half of a smaller whole.

*

Christianity hardly forms a unified subject matter. Its descent is quite obviously riven with rifts and diverging traditions. A pastoral motif can be traced nonetheless. Each incarnation of the Christian church shepherds its congregation, regulating the conduct of individual members on the grounds of their salvation. The pastorate has been a site of struggle admittedly, yet battles were fought over its direction and form rather than its existence as such.[41] 'There have been anti-feudal revolutions', so the argument goes, but there has never been 'an anti-pastoral revolution'. The pastorate has not yet experienced an insurrection so profound, or a revolution so far reaching that could have 'definitively expelled it from history'.[42] The 'soul' it cultivated, the promise of salvation it enshrined, the impossible pursuit of perfection it demanded; these 'instruments of torture' remain with us still.[43] That entire regime of power, one might say, is 'something from which we have still not freed ourselves'.[44] We do not question if education should adopt this framework at all. Rather, we ask, what kind of salvation should education offer? We attack education not for its continued adoption of an ethos of care, based on a promise of salvation. Rather, we attack education, if at all, for being the wrong kind of church, for failing to become the church it had the potential to be. In the eyes of its severest critics our school system adopts the form of 'a humble church built out of stones intended for a great cathedral. It is mocked by the scale of its unrealised potential, by the grandeur of the edifice that it might have been, if only its builders had not lost faith and gone into moral and political bankruptcy'. These critics 'beggar the school by projecting its structure as the flawed realisation of an ideal form'.[45] But the ideal form remains, and serves as a distraction from the real success story here. As we forever attack schools for failing to come up with the goods, for failing to deliver the salvation they promise, we refuse to see how the school has been more catastrophically successful than any cathedral; not in offering us salvation, but in making us forever beholden to that offer.

*

As a religious body the pastorate was rarely if ever in absolute control. Religious communities existed that countered the conduct of the pastorate with religious conduct of their own. [46] But this 'counter-conduct' (to borrow a term [47]) would refuse the priesthood without rejecting its form. Here the Protestant Reformation made resistance to the existing pastorate the principle of its replacement. Martin Luther attacked the established Church and its pastoral regime only to replace it with his own. As Nietzsche famously observed, Luther *'restored the church'* by attacking it.[48] Adopting the language of its adversaries, Luther declaimed against that 'pure invention' of the established Church – the spiritual divide it imposed between priesthood and laity. We are all 'consecrated priests through baptism', Luther pronounced. [49] A ridiculous suggestion for many, but Luther was content to be court jester. As he wrote, it was 'a question of who will put the bells on whom' – that is, who is the biggest fool. [50] Here Luther's Cynicism appears.[51] He was willing to adopt the guise of fool where necessary, for as it is said in the bible, and Luther quotes: 'He who wishes to be wise must become a fool'.[52] So let us sing along with Luther the 'fool's song' as he put it, and see what it means for the educator.[53] For Luther was looking far beyond his contemporary university – where 'loose living is practiced', where little is taught of the Christian faith, 'and where only the blind, heathen teacher Aristotle rules'.[54] Luther gave definition to an educational

Principles of Educational Sickness

Everyone is an educator, in theory, in the pastoral sense. Anyone can adopt a flock or individual, and make its care the basis of his own salvation. This is Luther's first educational principle.

*

Anyone can become an educator – for 'in cases of necessity anyone can baptize and give absolution'[55] – *but not everyone remains an educator.* Luther's second principle.

*

Whilst there is no 'higher consecration', no better calling, than that of educator who has Holy Scripture as his object: not all persons will hold this office. It should be considered 'an office', Luther tells us – rather than a secure identity guaranteed once and for all – since 'a priest in Christendom is nothing else but an officeholder'. He should be deposed, becoming 'a peasant or townsman like anybody else', if he is found wanting; for the devil's work is everywhere, all are susceptible to temptation. Cast aside here, along with the wayward priest, is 'the illusion that a priest can never be anything other than a priest, or ever become a layman. All this is just contrived talk, and human regulation'.[56] By analogy, the status of 'educator' like that of 'priest' should remain uncertain, it being contingent on the educator's good work. No teacher, and no priest is beyond dismissal. Remember, it is said: 'False teachers will rise up among you who will deceive you, and with their false and fanciful talk, will take advantage of you'.[57] This, highest office, must be under the constant gaze of its congregation. Against the Catholic position – which would exempt the clergy from the jurisdiction of civil courts – spiritual authority, Luther declares, is never beyond the temporal authority of its laity. None should be permitted to rise so far that they are beyond reach: 'Whoever is guilty, let him suffer.'[58]

*

Each teacher will have his congregation, but a following is forever contingent on the officeholder's faithful devotions. Luther's third principle.

*

I am faithful, the educator replies with rising intonation. My heart is with you: I adopt your best interests as my own.

*

The equivalence of all sheep and the paradox it brings is exaggerated by Luther and his kin, allowing the pastor not a moment's peace. In principle he could be replaced at any moment, and should fear as much. The pastor is a sheep like any other; his authority is only temporary. His burden, how he bears it, is his claim to excellence. It is his only claim, and a weak one at that, for the pastor's excellence is rather diminished by the diabolic realisation that in this world it is impossible to overcome sin. We are beyond indulgence and inescapably damned. Hence we should not become overly impressed by our own 'good works'.[59] And we must not, in a grander sense, become overly taken by this world either, for it is the Devil's dominion. We should not desire this world, and become influenced by our desire to live in it. Rather we should entertain with serious devotion a wish to die, for 'God makes alive by slaying'.[60] That is to say, we should pursue death, and 'death-in-life, in the hope of a more joyful resurrection'.[61] Our flesh belongs to the Devil, our spirit to Christ. In this latter doctrine we come to see 'the tremendous extension of the Devil's empire'. With Luther we realise how far God has 'retired into invisibility'[62] – leaving his elect more uncertain than ever as to the goodness of their efforts.

*

No teacher is good enough – no teacher can be good in the purest sense because education is a worldly thing – *but all must hope to become good*. Luther's fourth principle.

*

Luther accuses Rome of being so far gone, that 'if the pope were so scandalously bad as to lead crowds of souls to the devil, still he would not be deposed'.[63] This unquestioning guarantee of papal authority, this play of force, is denounced as a 'game of the Antichrist' or at any rate its forerunner.[64] The pope keeps a 'brothel above all imaginable brothels' in its extent and reach, Luther continues, for even the right to practice knavery must first be bought.[65] Anything that is forbidden can be permitted for a fee. Indulgences are for sale. The only absolute prohibition is to question papal authority itself. Papal authority operates as a regime of self-preservation. It will do the Devil's work if necessary to stay in power and shore up its riches. In that respect it is cynical to the extreme. As an educational force, the pastorate must define itself against such machinations. This much we may gather from Luther's polemic. The pastorate must defend itself by laying itself open. There is no earthly realm beyond reproach, no office beyond critique, it chants. If God spoke 'through an ass against a prophet, why should he not be able even now to speak through a righteous man against the pope'?[66] And in turn, why should he not at times speak through a pupil against his master?

*

We arrive at the following conclusion: I, Luther, am worthy of employment as your educator so long as I keep up my good work. For 'there is no authority in the church except to promote good'.[67] But my good work will never be good enough, for such is the human condition. So judge for yourselves, judge me by my faithful devotions, because I am your guide and as your guide I must be judged. Though remember, even as you find reason to depose me in this temporal realm, God remains my adjudicator. I have chosen to educate you, quite simply, because I keep the faith. That is all.

*

That is all? Was Luther's doctrine not hatched 'on the privy in the tower' – a position from which all accompanying sewage had egress down the monastery walls?[68] The *anality* of this vision, as Luther bestowed it from a great and precarious height, has not gone unnoticed.[69] Recurring here is a basic correlation between faith and vulnerability, where Luther becomes most ecstatic, proclaiming his principle of faith, precisely when crouched, when weakened by the matter at hand. We encounter faith as an expression of weakness. The force by which the educator pours out his devotions to education, is an expression of the frailty of both.[70]

Our Educational Conscience

*

The insidious logic of Luther's educator enables that figure to be elevated above us because he is precarious, because he has no other justification for his existence as your educator, than the argument that he is doing his best to be a good Christian (that he is busy with the matter at hand). As such, he comes from nowhere, assumes his office, and presumes a following. Because he has no independent claim to excellence beyond his faith, because he has, quite simply, and by virtue of his faith chosen to become an educator with all the precarity that position entails; he is to be considered excellent. That the educator is earnest and faithful in his devotions is his single most important qualification. The *passionate educator* is born here, in this moment.

*

Luther's philosophy may sound quaint to the modern ear. We know that in a century or so God would begin to perish. But the 'death of God' famously announced by Nietzsche still devastates us, even now. His absence is no more strongly felt than in the pious devotions of our contemporary secular humanist, or atheist, who considers himself to be above 'all that'. Our difficulty, is that despite all contenders, no candidate appears able to replace God as 'shared source of meaning and value'.[71] In the old language, we are left as before, with the entire devilry of the world, but without the possibility of escape or redemption. Caught short by a divine absence for which we are insufficiently prepared, we are forced to rely upon our habits, those 'habits of our senses'[72] now disconnected from their originating contexts. Thus struck, educators have only reproduced and extended the work of a medieval pastorate, adopting habits now divorced of sense. In modernity, education promises salvation, demands obedience, and requires as a condition of its functioning that each individual becomes known to its officeholders, where the care of all is considered dependent on the care of each. Nevertheless, the destination served by this regime has become uncertain. It has been obscured by the habitual belief in the existence of an educational good. By desperate habit we keep the faith.

*

Beware the promise of salvation in education. It perpetuates an entire 'economy of salvation' which plagues the secular realm as it does the religious, deriving from the medieval a belief that 'man was not made to live in this world' but was placed within it only so that he might pass into another.[73] He earns his salvation, deferring the realisation of his efforts to another realm. But that realm no longer exists before us as a definite promise. We defer as before, but do so without fixed horizons.

*

The end served by education is obscured by the habitual pursuit of a destination we presume worthy of our efforts. In the absence of a new rationale, one that would replace God and overcome this state of dependency that Christendom bequeaths us, old metaphysical doctrines, old destinations beyond physics (*meta ta physika*) are recycled as sufficient reason but without sufficient heart. The 'artificial respiration of old metaphysical doctrines'[74] forces a situation in which these doctrines are animated to serve the needs of a social reality in which they have no basis. Sensing this detachment, those who depend upon these doctrines develop a fanatical attachment to them. They consent to a kind of 'mass hypnosis'[75] that finds security in high principles, which constitute, so they believe, their last protection against nihilism. To live a principled existence, this is our last hope. To come across as principled is more important than the principles themselves, which can remain ill-defined. Education is one such principled fanaticism. With each fresh doubt, with each debasement of education, each demonstration that education is flawed, something independent is presumed more fervently to exist; some pure unadulterated core. This core attachment is all the more fervently protected as it is brought into question. Our attachment to education receives its strength from our fear of its debasement, its lack of value. Our fanatical attachment to this thing, education, is the product of our 'pessimistic gloom' – it is the effect of our weariness, fatalism and disappointment.[76]

*

Luther's fifth principle is lost on us: It represents the culmination of a philosophy we have yet to realise. We have no stomach for his more basic claim: 'I am the ripe shard and the world is the gaping anus.' Our vision of the world may be dark at times, but it is not as black as Luther's, for whom our only escape is *through* the digestive system of a world so corrupt that it is a 'rain of filth' upon us. 'We live in the Devil's worm-bag', Luther claims, and can only free ourselves by chasing it to the very bottom.[77] The imagery may be grotesque, but the point is acute. If we are to educate and retain, perhaps even foster, a belief in salvation through education, we must with determination and without recoil, hold in view the 'worm-bag' that constitutes education as our long confinement.

The Cynical Educator

V

MASS CYNICISM

Emptied Out and Set to Work
Our romantic educators may be impassioned, but passionate attachment is about all they have left. If Rousseau or Erasmus were resurrected, these 'fathers' of contemporary education, they would be rejected as impossible idealists. Even a famous pragmatist such as Dewey would be sniffed at for having his head in the clouds. Educational romanticism is an institutional affect.

*

'If someone wants to *seem* to be something, stubbornly and for a long time, he eventually finds it hard to *be* anything else.'[1] So argues Nietzsche. A doctor, for example, must seem the part in her patient's eyes, though she knows her professional expertise is made as much by rituals and habitual procedures, familiar scenarios and repeated phrases as by evidence-based practice. The educator faces a similar scenario. She must exude moral character and kindly intent, her techniques 'legitimated by reference to the notion that they will neither do harm to individuals or cause them frustration'.[2] To do away with the physical and subjective violence that education sometimes betrays, attempts are made to overlay this violence with 'the sweet smile' of forced harmony, 'in the protected island of an institution called 'school''. In this institution, it is fancied, 'problem-free relations' with children are possible if only one applies the 'right' principles.[3] The romantic educator believes in education, in the student, in the school. This educator remains hopeful and kindly, having our best interests at heart. Naturally in the staffroom and in private, educators may be biting and severe. Which reproduces that dissonance between the kindly appearance of education and its everyday disillusionment. At times such dissonance is keenly felt. Educational encounters are messy, testing, full of their own complex systems of injustice, and one suspects, rather damaging too. As an institution education suffers its glut of shifting imperatives. Educators face a task that appears all the more impossible for the hopes that are invested in it. But the educator must appear optimistic, stubbornly and with great resolve she acts the part, aligning herself to the idea education is synonymous with betterment. In this way the educator, who is aware of the hypocrisy of the caring professional, eventually out of desperation or exhaustion, sheds that hypocrisy, adopting the act that is performed. At least, this is what happens to the 'best' of us. There is a jaded remainder in the teaching profession. Their mass cynicism is not without its problems, but remains closest amongst contemporary cynicisms to actioning itself. For them I write, staking the terrain of a temptation that might still claim them, a temptation to believe in education once more. This temptation leads to a more duplicitous, less obvious cynicism, one that prevents discontent from engaging productively – which is to say actively – with its predicament. And so, when I write, I have those many teachers in mind who with jaw-clenched disgust, despise everything that education represents today. Those who would, given the chance, trample underfoot each new government initiative. Those who look with barely disguised contempt, if not open hostility, at managers, educational consultants, school advisors, improvement officers, and presiding academics. These agents and agencies are rightly despised for their constant meddling. The teaching profession is ground down, without space to breathe. But there is a more dangerous effect, more dangerous than compression, more disturbing than 'outside' pressures such as audit, managerial imposition, or consumer dissatisfaction. This danger takes hold as teachers and lecturers are encouraged to come up for air, to have faith once more. This invitation to hope promotes a weakened, weakening cynicism. It exploits and puts to work the last remaining educational commitments of an otherwise broken workforce. This far more duplicitous cynicism, leads to final exhaustion and drains that workforce of its last remaining pleasure: Revolt.

*

In modern secular institutions faith is instrumentalised and our cynicism is set to work. Following Peter Sloterdijk, we might take Dostoyevsky's Grand Inquisitor as its prototype.[4] As Sloterdijk explains, this Inquisitor may appear as a figure of the Christian Middle Ages, but functions as a retrospective projection. He represents a more recent, secular cynicism. Dostoyevsky describes the return of Christ, arriving in Seville where the Spanish Inquisition is busying itself with heretics. Christ performs a number of miracles, ending by the Cathedral as an open child's coffin is 'borne with weeping into the place of worship'. Christ speaks and the seven-year-old girl sits upright, holding the bouquet she was to be buried with. There is a bit of a to-do, and then the Cardinal Grand Inquisitor himself appears, with his 'withered face and sunken eyes'.[5] He raises an index finger and orders the arrest. The Cardinal recognises his captive as Christ, and commits him to be burned at the stake. As Sloterdijk interprets: 'What Jesus had assumed about his crucifiers as grounds for forgiveness – "for they know not what they do" – can in no way be applied to the churchman. He knows what he is doing and he knows it with downright shocking clarity'.[6] The Cardinal accuses Jesus of disrupting the work of the Catholic Church, which is, he explains, stamping out 'the last sparks of Christian freedom'. The Church is making amends for a cruel mistake: Christ encouraged his followers to seek freedom, and thereby set them up to fail. It was a callous move, causing so much pain and suffering. The Cardinal explains how the Church was forced to respond. It satisfied the needs of the majority – who require security, habit, certainty and tradition before all else – by siding with and sacrificing itself to the Devil. Out of compassion the Church inflicted order, power and law upon those without the strength to be free, whilst convincing them of their liberty, hammering a rhetoric of freedom into their heads. This sacrifice, this pact with the Devil, is what gives the Cardinal his 'unhappy consciousness'. But all was done in the knowledge 'millions of people will enjoy their existence' as a result of the security spiritual dominion assures.[7] The Cardinal's faith was emptied out, rationalised and put to work.

*

The bold and barefaced cynicism of the Grand Inquisitor is too heroic for us to quite believe. His strain of unchristian Christianity has gone too far even for modern cynics to stomach. To build benevolent rule upon an evil lie is too much. At best – and this is Sloterdijk's point – we cynics have only 'one foot in the area beyond good and evil,' feeling around with the other for a reassuring foothold in morality. Our modern cynical consciousness seeks to combine 'a rigorous *cynicism of means* with an equally rigid *moralism of ends'*. As far as ends are concerned, scarcely anyone risks imagining 'a real region beyond good and evil – for that would be 'nihilism." Consequent attempts to resist the accomplishment of nihilism have, for Sloterdijk, constituted 'the real ideological war of modernity.'[8] It is precisely here that the bloodless romanticism of contemporary education takes hold, with its vague moralism of ends. The educational ideal this romanticism serves becomes an ever-retreating formation, an empty signifier, and a distant prospect. However brutal educational institutions might become as means to an end, education itself – 'the ultimate end' – remains untarnished. Peter Sloterdijk recommends the following: An equally deep-set Cynicism of ends must accompany the cynicism of means that characterizes our present. This Cynicism of ends would reveal the 'fundamental excess and absurdity'[9] of goals ever retreating before us. This condition of perpetual deferral, where we have always just one more matter to attend to, one more wish to satisfy, one more account to settle, is 'what keeps the system of excessive production going'. We are haunted by ends that delude us with their distant light, for 'whenever we approach it recedes once more into the distance.'[10] Mass cynicism is overcome only by its intensification, by dialogue with the nihilism it is symptomatic of.

Our Detached Negativity

Our cynicism becomes manifest in the workplace refrain, *I'm just playing the game*, where most would admit they play to a tune not always their own. A decidedly weak cynicism of means, this cynicism of ours is far more diffuse than we realise, occurring where we least expect. We find it too in that rigid moralism of ends which afflicts education. This moralism would immobilise us completely. It would be our educational rigor mortis, if our bodies were not already broken into so many pieces.

*

Refusing to take itself or anything else in earnest, contemporary cynicism cannot be attacked by conventional means. Diffuse and insubstantial, it runs circles around sincere discussion. As Sloterdijk observes, paid up philosophers long struggled to comprehend 'the ideological template' of such 'unserious, shallow systems' preferring more serious opponents.[11] Academic research is similarly wrong-footed. If cynicism can be attacked at all, a different style of delivery is required.

*

Cynics were once eccentrics, ridiculing social convention, attacking the high-minded values and commitments of civilized life, emulating their most notorious representative Diogenes. Cynicism made its way into the Roman Empire as a popular philosophy, a scurrilous way of life for the 'disenfranchised and discontented'.[12] But Cynicism held its attractions for the educated too. Well-to-do Romans would co-opt Cynicism as a respectable philosophy, and turn it into a literary genre. Many centuries later Cynicism underwent a kind of revival. Marshalled to the project of Enlightenment, a literary, respectable Cynicism was put to use by those attempting (in the 'spirit' of Diogenes) to deface select political norms and traditions.[13] Returned in sanitised form, its most scurrilous and scatological elements carefully excised, Cynicism was so 'flattened' by co-option to the spirit of Enlightenment that it was diminished to insignificance.[14] A neutered philosophical tradition could now be rejected on terms other than its own. It was condemned 'theoretically unfit' – a nonsensical rationale from the Cynic perspective – and marginalised by the standards of newly professionalised philosophy.[15] A militant Cynicism all but disappeared, leaving behind a few surface features, mere imprints incorporated within our modern cynic attitude. This jaded attitude so extended the critique of tradition inaugurated by Enlightenment thinkers, that even their legacies are now cynically attacked. Modern cynicism can be described as the final resting place of 'an exhausted critical consciousness' that has finally consumed itself.[16] On occasion this modern attitude is expressed with force, as a kind of morally disillusioned, politically disaffected contempt for the ideals and promises of modernity.[17] Generally though, cynicism appears in disguise, as a harried attachment to those same ideals. These ideals remain with us as surface commitments, commitments for the sake of commitment, enacted to be believed.

*

The split between ancient Cynicism and its cynical heirs has only compounded and rendered more exacting any attempt at revival. Who could recall Cynicism from its slumber? Its descendant namesake has such widespread influence it is hard to shake off. This mass cynicism has given up the quirks and outrages of its ancestral tradition. Banal yet oddly formidable, it sidesteps all attackers, not by insult or gall, but through insipid wet contempt. It will not be called short for perpetuating errors, because it no longer pays reverence to the truth. Having given up on reason, modern cynics kneel no more before its promise, claiming that reason has been overtaken by the "power of things".[18] The attitude of contemporary cynicism is near insensible to attack, responding to any serious combatant with an air of ironic detachment.

*

The cynic is able to survive, indeed thrive despite persistent doubt, a nagging realisation the activities we engage in must fail to live up to their expectations. For want of alternatives, the cynic learns to accommodate himself to, if not 'implicate himself in the very system he has damned'.[19] The cynic often remains in work, working the system. Modern cynics know what they are doing but do it anyway, if they didn't someone else would.

*

Contemporary cynics claim to have discarded all illusions. They have seen the world without its ideological gloss: 'it is all really about money/power/sex', they declare. But this 'realism without illusions is the very form of their blindness'. They will not see how their cynicism is itself an operation of power; it functions to maintain the system they deride. That, precisely, is the naivety of their cynical wisdom, its blindness to itself.[20] As heirs of Enlightenment they finally decide; "we are enlightened, we are apathetic". In such contexts 'no one talks anymore of a *love* of wisdom', we are only left with its motions.[21]

*

'Because everything has become problematic, everything is also somehow a matter of indifference'.[22] Having been 'schooled in reality', contemporary cynics have 'grown up' to embrace it.[23] The ideological commitments of modernity are half-believed or dismissed in displays of light-hearted disdain. Either way these hopes are no longer taken in earnest. Modern cynics are not fatally disillusioned, and refuse to be dragged down by a reality laid bare. At worst they are a little listless, having been rescued from depression by a 'detached negativity', which 'scarcely allows itself any hope, at most a little irony and pity'.[24] From this perspective everything is hopeless, yet the cynic refuses to become genuinely depressed. Present-day cynics are only 'borderline melancholics'.[25] Despite everything they have seen and done, they remain more or less able to work. Desperate for work, determined to survive, propelled by an instinct for self-preservation, the cynic puts up with dubious situations, and finally carries out their business.

*

Melancholia afflicts those who know not what they have lost.[26] Melancholic cynics feel a sense of loss, and feel entitled to indulge themselves in that sensation, without having a clear picture of what life was like before the loss occurred. A phantom of the past, or of the present that might have been, takes hold. A world better ordered by reason, or by a more genuine commitment to justice, or by a more coherent community, or by a better sense of collective purpose, is bemoaned. In educational settings these ideological 'losses' are matched if not exceeded by the personal losses of those who joined the profession with more immediate but equally hazy desires, such as the hope for job satisfaction, the anticipation of meaningful work, and the wish to 'make a difference'. Lacking clear conception of these lost ideals, educators will not come to terms with their departure. Here they are prone to a deeper and more enduring melancholy. Not only do they fail to confront their loss, they risk internalising the lost object to prevent its departure.[27] Melancholic educators of this sort are subjectively wedded to educational ideals that are for all intents and purposes lost causes. These lost causes are retained half-alive but in a putrescent state, existing as vague subjective attachments. Educators are prevented thereby from coming to terms with a loss that is everywhere apparent but rarely confronted. They remain attached to ideals that are everywhere inoperable.[28] With these lost ideals internalised and thereby 'retained', educators inherit all the ambivalence once built into educational goods that were promised but forever deferred. Abandoned by educational contexts that have fallen under the yoke of instrumentalism, melancholic educators are rendered susceptible to the belief they are the last true educators standing. This becomes their romanticism. They defend individuated educational goods as if they were their last representatives. Educators hereby internalise all the pain of a good that is promised but never appears. Our best educators see themselves as the last defenders of a good they cannot finally manifest, or excrete, a good whose content they cannot adequately describe. A little overstuffed with commitments but otherwise reflexively buffered, these educators remain at work, a bit dejected and troubled but not fundamentally disturbed. It would seem their 'coming to terms' requires far more than an acknowledgement of their educated nihilism. It necessitates a careful, meticulous and sustained effort to disentangle subjective attachments that bind us to education still. We put ourselves, with education, on the block.

The Educator's Smile

As an institution, education is widely attacked for its cynicisms, plagued by activities that are openly performative and often rather faddish. Of little value in themselves some claim, their meaning derives from the bureaucratic or governmental ethos to which they are subservient. This wider ethos serves equally specious masters such as the imagined needs of an economy in perpetual flux. Confused about how one best feeds the temperamental impulses of global capital, education retreats to a focus on skills malleable by definition, and adaptable thereby to uncertain contexts.

*

Educators are as cynical as the best of us, sometimes openly so. The hollow-eyed teacher, ground down and grim faced, under pressure and failing, is familiar on screen and in daily life. This teacher has become distant from the profession and the things it has her do. Ironically detached, avoiding the pain otherwise produced by more heartfelt commitments, such a teacher has long given up on the job, yet does it anyway.

*

It is hard to exaggerate the plight of educators, operating in a realm whose airs once tasted sweet. Education has been ploughed over, upturned by widely recognised forces variously denounced as the reductive powers of commodification, audit, managerialism, performativity and that abstract beast, 'neoliberalism'. Educational researchers have bemoaned such attackers for decades, yet few admit in their wake the situation has become, as it strikes me, decidedly post-apocalyptic. This refusal to admit the full consequences of educational destruction is extraordinary, since it is clear enough that for some conditions have become intolerable. Educators are quitting the profession in droves, sometimes rather publicly, writing embittered, valedictory articles and emails, even suicide notes.[29] Whilst those remaining in the profession are themselves often also despondent, they may resist giving up hope entirely. Their optimism may be at times forced, but is a force to be reckoned with. A romantic urge lives on in the profession, and tempts even those most dejected. It is manifested in the commitments of those educators who will not give up on the idea theirs is a noble cause. For today's cynic is often a romantic too, though of a peculiar kind: When educational ideals are resurrected, they appear in a cluster, hiding behind one another for mutual support. When mentioned they are accompanied by the sound of swallowing, betraying lack of conviction.

*

Let us consider the value of our highest educational values. I suspect *'education as an emancipatory endeavour'*, would strike many as a little over the top these days. We in the liberal West believe ourselves largely emancipated already. *'Education in pursuit of social justice'* receives far more attention, but is divorced from the dream that social roles could be allocated on merit and wealth could be fundamentally redistributed. The realisation of that old dream became harder and harder to imagine as sociologists explained with evermore sophistication how inequalities are subtly reproduced. The aspiration to achieve social justice effectively killed itself as a result of its own truthfulness.[30] Finally in an age of 'impact' and 'knowledge exchange', *'education for its own sake'* is only guiltily admitted as an ideal, for it bears the whiff of its aristocratic origins. It is tainted by association with wealth and leisure, falling under the shadow of its very own ivory tower.

*

Today's educator adopts a fixed but miserable grin, at once despairing yet hopeful. I feel the misery of this educator most acutely at university meetings, where depressed resignation to institutional and political imperatives holds sway. Here comes yet another drive to secure the financial future of our employer, and by clear implication ours too, through higher student recruitment, better reputation, more research funding, and so on. At times we discuss little else, falling prematurely between the wheels of that juggernaut, which seems to be squeezing any space left for thought, and thoughtful teaching, from our working lives. This despair is most acutely expressed as a kind of desperation, where colleagues grasp anything at hand that may give them purpose. For this reason, vapid institutional drivers towards a more 'inspirational student experience' (for the sake of fees), or more 'world class research' (for the sake of funding), are rarely greeted with the open contempt they deserve. Some academics find themselves rather drawn to these imperatives, perhaps despite their better judgement, hoping against hope to find something in them worth rescuing. Faced with a landscape of defeated ideals, the educator who does not quit the profession retreats into her educational present. Abandoned by educational ideals, devoid of values to which they can appeal yet believing themselves undervalued, romantic educators shroud themselves in the beneficent aura they take such pains to cultivate. They devote themselves to the job and allow themselves to imagine their efforts are not in vain.

The Educator's Last Hope

An old educational ethos stretches to modernity but extends only weakly to our present: 'The more arduous the duty one assumes, the more it educates and uplifts the soul', it repeats.[31] For contemporary tastes this declaration is a little too lofty in tone if not a trifle contrived. Today it is sufficient to call an arduous task *educational* and be done. In that way the labour of educating and being educated is exalted by simple decree. This completes the short circuit that connects the assumed educational good with its often compromised reality. 'It is educational,' we say in all simplicity. Indeed some educators will put up with almost any debasement however technocratic and instrumental so long as it can be rendered formative, and hence educational. To which the Cynic reply: Formative of what?

*

Today hopeful educators scarcely allow themselves to believe education will change the world. They hold fast to Bernstein's edict: 'education cannot compensate for society'.[32] Yet refusing to abandon the profession and their professional identity as a progressive force, they remain resolutely positive. They focus on the plight of the moment, on the plight of those before them. For the hope of the educator cannot be sustained in abstraction. The idea hers is a benevolent profession, that it is essentially good, requires propping up. Abandoned by educational ideals, the benevolent educator needs something concrete on which to cling. For this reason, initiatives launched by government and sponsored by business promising to deliver us to an educational good, hold a certain attraction. These initiatives trade on over-inflated and often politicised and commercialised promises of hope, happiness, individual wellbeing, economic prosperity and collective security. They are not uniformly adopted, nor are they implemented without adjustment. When they are not met with open hostility, or enacted with begrudging compliance, or adopted in an effort to survive the system; when they generate some interest and some measure of support, their success where it occurs is not the simple product of pragmatic calculation or managerial imposition. The hold of techniques promising to deliver value to the educational project draws strength from the felt need they satisfy. Their promise is to redeem education through its adoption of fresh innovations.

Clearly this redemptive promise is unevenly felt, being more alluring to those in managerial or advisory positions. But where these innovations succeed most they feed an educational desire that is committed to a project of educational redemption whilst being profoundly pessimistic about the possibility of its realisation. In this desperate search for hope and meaning we encounter once more the effects of our longer battle with nihilism. According to the logic of that battle, once God the former giver of value departs, principles of universal happiness, reason, justice and humanity are slipped in. This sleight of hand takes place without bringing into question the entire evaluative framework it perpetuates. Values are still placed above and beyond us, against which we remain all too human. Given this cycle of disappointment is so old, and given its workings have long been revealed, since Nietzsche that is, it is tempting to suggest an escape. We might abandon this metaphysic altogether and build values from the bottom up. But metaphysical attachments haunt us still; they are not done away with by decree. And besides, this 'solution' is already anticipated by government. Whilst transcendent educational values have become increasingly anaemic in their effects, they have not been replaced by other grand principles that would prevent us from experiencing the agony and bewilderment which descends as old values begin to decay. This sense of loss is prevented rather differently now through the educational narcotic of constant activity. We take some small measure of 'delight in bustling about', though our delight expresses the 'restless energy of a haunted mind'.[33] This sense of loss, experienced when transcendent values become doubtful, we abate through the ceaseless adoption of work, work initiatives and accompanying techniques. We hate these initiatives, but we love them too. For the loss of value that afflicts education is papered over by such movement. Values are today constructed *in situ* through the everyday reality of educational work. Which is not to say that educators are increasingly duped by the system, that they are distracted by the day-to-day and thereby diverted from the pursuit of something more meaningful, more educational even. Given form in motion, in the daily commitments of a workforce on the brink of exhaustion, the educational good has never been more literal.

*

The erosion of faith in higher educational values is not experienced as acutely as it might be, since educational values are already brought down to earth. Values are embodied in the various activities and techniques available to education, techniques that instrumentalise our hopes, fears, vulnerabilities and emotions. Educators have come to embody the value these tools create through use. In this way, instead of working towards the fulfilment of transcendent ideals, educators *give value* to their work, through work. Even grumbling about work becomes an activity of self-affirmation; it implies work is worth grumbling about. When transcendent ideals are lost, educators become more committed to the job, not less.[34]

*

The educational critic might pay heed: When attacking that constant barrage of fresh imperatives, new techniques and 'essential' procedures, that perpetual drive for 'improvement'[35] which defines our educational landscape, dominating today's classroom, school and university with its whirlwind of initiatives, do not ask: How do they warp the educational endeavour, distort it, distract it, and so on. Rather, investigate how they promise to give education meaning, value and substance through their adoption and use; ask what desires they satisfy, what temptations they permit. For the great curiosity of contemporary education is that hope and belief limp on.

*

The pursuit of hope in education takes different forms.[36] Where pupils are encouraged to 'reach for their dreams', they are expected to hope resolutely. Impossible hopes are sometimes indulged, but must be managed through their subdivision into achievable steps. Here a mode of hoping is adopted that is carefully goal-directed and guided by more realistic objectives. Pupils are encouraged to live by their predicted grades, and aspire to hopes that have been judged statistically sound. Sound hopes such as these are then to be combined with far less well-defined, less goal-directed, more patiently hopeful dispositions. These reflect the attitude of the profession, which is beholden to a patient optimism. It makes a virtue of this distinctly quiet, self-contained form of hoping. Archetypal traits associated with the good student – such as modesty, humility, perseverance, restraint and self-discipline – are recycled and invested with new meaning. They are attached to pedagogies that seek to educate pupils in modes of hoping that will better accommodate them to the possibilities and opportunities afforded by the existing social order. With the activity of hoping chastened in this way, pupils learn to live in hope, and educators learn to place their hope in those they educate.

*

From the resolutely positive stance of the motivational educator, that saviour of the educational present, open cynicism is likened to 'a plague that kills dreams'. Strategies are recommended to help teachers 'stop cynical feelings', including the adoption of a 'hopeless student', because 'it is hard to be cynical when someone depends upon you, especially a child'. As if everyday educational cynicism could be defeated by a love of the student that would transcend into a desire to secure 'hope for all'.[37] But the motivational educator is a false radical, and a concealed cynic. For there is nothing inherently radical, or even progressive, about the pursuit of hope. Capitalism depends upon it. Advanced liberal societies operate by stimulating rather than simply directing or repressing the desires of their populations. Under these conditions, obedient subjects are those who do *not* give up hope.

*

Like hope, fear has its uses. Our fears are redefined as vulnerabilities, and in that form they are adopted. It is striking how a discourse of vulnerability tempts the pastoral teacher into compliance, where policies and professional activities bring to visibility an ever-expanding range of mundane incidents and feelings that indicate our susceptibility to harm. The various symptoms of vulnerability, and the various techniques, possibilities and sites for intervention it proposes, have multiplied.[38] In Britain, the poor, the infirm, the disabled and the exploited have all been reconceptualised as vulnerable subjects. They are viewed in terms of the risks they face, and the risks they pose to society. Young people, who may be all of the above but also have the disadvantage of their youth, are said to occupy a particularly precarious position.[39] Various agencies committed to social welfare, or social order, engage our vulnerabilities at this level, responding to those factors that are felt to make lives precarious. But the perspectives they adopt, however well meaning in appearance, are decidedly pessimistic. The possibility of a more secure, less risky future is all they can imagine. The risks posed by social and institutional life are viewed as perpetual threats we must learn to negotiate. Education must teach us to better cope with the inevitable disappointments of life, developing our ability to adapt and mould ourselves to changing contexts. Whilst institutions promising to develop such skills may appear positive, they are nonetheless despairing. They preach an ethic of survival in an unpredictable and dangerous world.

*

The melancholic underpinnings of contemporary education are hidden in part by attempts to appear positive. With determination we might sound out this teacherly attitude. Following Nietzsche, educators might again philosophise with a hammer blow, listening to the sounds that return.[40] But that would miss the point and misdiagnose the problem. When our idols are no longer becoming hollow but are produced through frenetic activity, we do not tap at them, deftly and with determination so as to hear and make heard their empty reverberations. Our idols may be insubstantial, but they are not hollow in any straightforward sense. Akin to egg timers that are turned and turned again – it matters not which way the sand falls, so long as it flows. A tapping at, or even a destruction of such idols would be futile. They are mass-produced. With their coming obsolescence built-in, these idols loose value as soon as they arrive.

*

The effects of accumulated wealth have been something of a disappointment. We in the West guiltily admit more wealth does not always entail more happiness. Deemed to be facing a crisis in happiness,[41] psychologists and 'psychologically minded' individuals multiply in such a climate.[42] They tap into and support a proliferation of magazines, self-help manuals, life coaches, professional interests, educational techniques, whole-school policies and political reforms. Proponents of a happy life generously adopt the role of educators, educating us to help ourselves to a life of greater contentment. In this context, certain mythological constructs, such as the happy marriage,[43] the happy family,[44] the happy childhood,[45] or the happy consumer, are recycled and imposed as aspirational objects. Happiness becomes contingent, a promise attached to objects of desire. And guilt is produced in those inevitable moments when happiness does not arrive as promised. We become isolated at moments such as these, wondering why we feel empty, asking what prevented the promise from finding its fulfilment. We feel inadequate, questioning not the promise but our ability to enjoy.[46] Some react with determined cheerfulness.[47] Not in itself a problem, necessarily. But a cheerful attitude risks becoming a moral duty, where those who abstain are not simply pitied for their lack of good cheer, they are resented for letting the rest of us down. Good cheer becomes the individual's contribution to collective wellbeing.[48] The cynicism of happiness, then, is that it is either rendered remote and unrealisable, or immediate and insistent. In the first case, the pursuit of happiness isolates individuals, suggesting they are unable to live up to a collective ideal of what it means to be happy. In the second case, where individuals are brought together in good cheer, the emotional condition that unites them becomes an imperative for others. It is tempting, as one faces up to a climate of forced cheer and happiness, to respond by adopting their opposites. Those seeking to resist on these terms would of course be promptly dismissed simply because of their gloom. For there is today 'a kind of mortgage' on thinking that proceeds in a negative direction. So we put it off, suffering 'a self-imposed obligation to arrive at a cheerful conclusion'.[49] It is considered enough of an accusation to declare that someone lacks hope, that they have nothing to promise, nothing positive to contribute, to dismiss them from the scene of debate. But this dismissal is symptomatic of an embedded cynicism. Against it, instead of patching 'the cracks in the edifice of our civilization', we might emancipate ourselves from our 'fear of despair', from 'the fear of being called nihilistic', and be prepared to face up to the darkness of our times.[50]

*

Gloomy educators have their merits, better placed to resist the use of positive emotion as a governing technique. Yet there are dangers inherent in a leaden response. It risks perpetuating a common mistake, where we take the pursuit of happiness at its own word. Hence those reacting with a determined effort to become relentlessly severe, even manifestly gloomy, might do so only after recognising the deep pessimism and disavowed cynicism of those promoting emotional positivity. Those attempting a gloomy rebellion would point rather insistently to the pessimism of educators still cleaving to the remote hope of educational redemption. The unique claim of revolting individuals such as these would be that they, unlike others, have come to terms with their melancholia.

*

As an educational objective the pursuit of happiness, or wellbeing, achieves its appeal against the common-sense view that educational institutions have become anything but happy, that they are dominated by the miserable pursuit of results. Hence the allure of an industry which divides happiness into teachable techniques that presume to make the pursuit of it more realistic. We must identify such activities without equivocation as survival techniques, designed to accommodate us to our late modern predicament. In no particular order: we wonder how we might survive capitalism, overwork and underemployment; global warming, environmental degradation and depleted resources; the other, one another and ourselves. In this context, happiness does not fulfil the role of a transcendental ideal. When it appears as such, this is part of its technique. Reduced to the status of a survival objective, happiness is rendered subservient to a biopolitical ethos that pursues 'health' against 'ill health', rather than 'right' against 'wrong'. The pursuit of happiness becomes an issue of success or failure, evading all questions concerning the legitimacy or illegitimacy, and hence value of the quest itself.[51] In its operationalized form, taken as a set of handy, learnable techniques, this educational activity is, again, intrinsically pessimistic and inherently cynical. It separates happiness as an affective state from a more critical and serious engagement with the problem of happiness. For some, the most obvious alternative would be a revived Aristotelian approach that redefines happiness by associating it with the ability to live a good and flourishing life. The advantage of this definition is that it ties the question of happiness to a consideration of the context in which it is to be realised. We should, however, avoid any nostalgia for classical versions of the good life that were themselves connected to systems of coercion, also excluding by default the vast majority of the population as incapable of its realisation. Still, we can observe a contrast here with modern happiness, which is to be treated on its own without bringing into question the perfectibility of the way of life to which it is connected. As we late moderns are so fond of admitting, our way of life is beyond fundamental adjustment. This life may be imperfect but we are nevertheless stuck with it. Trapped as we are in the present, we must simply do our best to enjoy what we have accumulated.

The Educator's Last Breath

Contemporary cynicism is widespread but hard to detect. Increasingly 'lived as a private disposition', today's cynics do not generally announce themselves, having little energy or appetite for direct confrontation. They are too well integrated into the society they scorn, existing as a diffuse but hardly rebellious presence. Contemporary cynics have no wish to appear eccentric. It is quite difficult indeed to bring this 'diffuse, murky cynicism to expression'. 'It has withdrawn into a mournful detachment' and 'no longer sees any reason to expose itself aggressively'.[52] In its educational contexts cynicism is particularly shy. It lies hidden within the educator's good intentions. Facing such widespread disavowal, the standard response of the educational critic is to subject educators to some form of ideology critique. This would systematically diagnose their disorder and explain how education today, in practice, betrays its ideals, and unwittingly promotes ends most educators would not openly support. The educational enterprise would be attacked as somehow degenerate, as if a true education could then emerge. But if the cynicism of education is as widespread as I suggest, this kind of ideology critique will have no great effect. Otherwise put, our problem is *not that we are fools* in need of enlightenment. Rather, our problem is that *we lack the power not to be fooled*.[53] It is comparatively easy to be critical of society and claim that we are not taken in by it. The problem we face is located at a different level. To borrow once more a phrase from Nietzsche, our difficulty as critics is that we live in 'a society that no longer has the strength to *excrete*' those commitments and values it finds dubious.[54] In such a climate, the cynical educator must be invited to embrace *and force out* a widespread cynicism that is everywhere in practice, but rarely admitted.

*

The cynical educator is challenged to admit the crisis of value from which we suffer, 'without perishing'[55] and without ceasing to educate. The task is to embrace a crisis of value that is everywhere apparent but rarely acknowledged and even less often accepted. It is to reject the commitment to work, to perpetual industry. It is to attack an educational injunction that would have us give education value through our exhaustion as a labour force.

VI

INSULTS AND OBSCENITIES

Scandalous Teachings
Contemporary cynicism lacks conviction, accommodating itself to the status quo it rejects. This attitude has but a sinuous link to its ancient Greek ancestor, which refused point blank to accommodate itself to anything or anyone.

*

Educators are not always teachers, and teachers do not have to believe in education. The ancient Cynics were a case in point, pushing any definition of education to its limits by turning it into an insult. Diogenes of Sinope actively ridiculed those who would have him be their teacher. According to one account: 'When someone expressed a wish to study philosophy with him, Diogenes gave him a fish to carry and told him to follow in his footsteps; the man threw it away out of shame. When

Diogenes came across him some time later, Diogenes burst out laughing and said, 'Our friendship was brought to an end by a fish!'[1] What the man failed to understand is that to practice Cynicism one undergoes repeated humiliation, where to carry the fish (or cheese in a different version of the story), would be to act as if one were Diogenes' slave. The Cynic has a taste for humiliation, understanding that shame is 'the most intimate social fetter, which binds us, *before* all concrete rules of conscience, to universal standards of behaviour'.[2]

*

Even from a distance of more than two millennia, it is hard to take Cynicism entirely seriously; the Cynic responds to seriousness with malicious laughter. Cynic humour is designed to outrage its victims, since outrage expresses the very conventions the Cynic seeks to upset.[3]

*

The Cynic scoffs at the very notion of an educated soul; *your* educated soul. The Cynic sneers at the entire history of Western education. For it bears the imprint of transcendental Platonism which put this phantom into circulation. Under this philosophical tread, education became synonymous with activities seeking to control one's appetites in the name of a 'higher' calling. Since these appetites were taken to be a private, if not shameful weakness of the untrained soul, education was developed as a specialist pursuit requiring intimacy, seclusion and trust. Again, the Cynic snorts with contempt. For the Cynic there is no retreat to a secluded spot, or inner citadel. Cynics seek exposure, living on the street, begging and then berating any would-be benefactors. The shamelessly licentious, happily impoverished, barely dressed Cynic finds all higher things to be worthless and says so, pushing courage and boldness 'to the point that it becomes intolerable insolence'.[4] The Cynic breaks with the world of convention and forces it to react.

*

Foucault devoted his last lectures to ancient Cynicism. Here he elaborated on the term *parrhesia,* meaning to speak freely, now using it to define the Cynic philosopher. The term applies to others too, such as Socrates who conducted free speech as dialogue. But unlike Socrates, a Cynic such as Diogenes of Sinope (known for masturbating in public amongst other things[5]) would not be so courteous. His speech would pour forth heedless of whether or not one consented to its onslaught, requiring courage of a different sort. Whilst Socrates risked the irritation if not anger of his companions by persuading them through dialogue, trickery and irony of their ignorance, of not knowing what they claimed to know, the Cynic risks the vengeance of his auditors berating them to reject and despise everything they accept to be true and proper. Dialogue is replaced by diatribe and insult, or it is suspended altogether, whereupon one exhibits oneself shamelessly before a public, causing deliberate offence. Where Socratic irony sought to create a sense of existential doubt amongst friends and acquaintants, the Cynic brought forth a public scandal.

*

It is claimed that after one particularly well-received public oration, at which 'many stood about and listened to his words with great pleasure', Diogenes ceased speaking, and 'squatting on the ground, performed an indecent act'.[6] This caused great insult. Diogenes not only excreted, he did so precisely when his audience was most enraptured.

*

Wisdom is associated with a metaphor of elevation. The wise rise above the workaday diversions of the rest and refine themselves. Entire cultures view themselves in this way, each becoming taken by its own sophistication. So when the Cynic shits openly he insults an audience in denial, for it shits too. The consequence of denial for those dissociating themselves from what is low and embarrassing, is that they eventually end up 'suffocating in their own shit', as Sloterdijk phrased it.[7] They are overcome by nausea as they encounter the base matter their highest achievements are built of. The Cynic, by contrast, is not overcome by paralysis, having become familiar with his raw materials.

*

Cynics left the labour of writing up their exploits and sayings to others. They handed down no set texts and established no firm doctrines.[8] Theirs was an attitude and a way of being, rather than a philosophy in the conventional sense. Indeed the Cynic had contempt for the formal lectures and exalted language of established philosophy. The Cynic 'who simply regards such dialogue as hot air – passes wind by way of a critique'.[9]

Bawdy Educators

When approaching the Cynics we are forced to rely upon a range of sketches and sayings of doubtful authenticity. These were passed down by commentators wedded to other modes of address, who were not always sympathetic to a Cynic way of life.[10] Early commentators found themselves face to face with a philosophy that addressed a wider, and hence in their eyes, 'not very cultured public', drawing its recruits 'from outside the educated elites that usually practiced philosophy'.[11] Some claimed Cynics were mere opportunists. These rude upstarts were crude imitators, pretending to cultivate a philosophy, but succeeding only in the cultivation of their ignorance.[12] Others accused Cynics of a kind of barbarity, hell bent on destroying all beauty, honesty and goodness, trampling justice and honour under foot, devoid of respect for the rights of others, operating without reverence for the Gods, and perhaps worst of all, turning philosophy into a laughing stock.[13] Those adopting a Cynic way of life surely deserved stoning, if not the *barathrum*. They should be thrown into this Athenian pit just like any other criminal so it could swallow up and devour their profanity.[14] Such violent loathing and devout retching over the shameless existence of lowbrow Cynicism, nevertheless served a recuperative function for the scandalised. It allowed Roman commentators to distance themselves from the noisy and coarse realities of a Cynic life, so they might reclaim another 'measured, thoughtful, well-bred, discreet, honest and really austere Cynicism'.[15] This high-class Cynicism was a respectable philosophy one might practice at home. Bold but honourable, here was a Cynicism one could base in reading and careful reflection. This was a Cynicism good enough for the educated. A Cynic of this variety would still speak the truth, fearlessly at times, but without the insults and aggressions of the Cynic diatribe. Such insights would be carefully delivered and could expect to be well received. Indeed the Cynic in question would finally gain the respect of his fellow citizens. Most of all, he would be admired for his consistency, for how closely his words matched his deeds, where his philosophy was demonstrated through his actions first and foremost. This honourable Cynic was incapable of hypocrisy. He would always be true to his word.

*

The street Cynic was a familiar sight under Roman rule. Cynicism of this type had to be categorically rejected if anything was to be rescued for respectable philosophy. Hence Epictetus' quip, that street Cynics 'mimicked their masters in nothing other than cutting farts'.[16] Such bawdy imitators were to be ignored: In the fourth century, Emperor Julian devoted some time to the study of Cynicism. He was prompted by the influence street Cynics were having on his soldiers and lower levels of citizenry.[17] Deeply irritated by their activities, Julian explores how a 'true' Cynicism might operate. Accordingly, the body is looked down upon as 'that jailer of the soul'[18] to be escaped through rigorous training. It becomes something the Roman Cynic learns to 'utterly despise' and regard as 'more deserving to be thrown out than dung'.[19] The Cynic learns to control his passions, and ensure he will never again be ruled by his 'nether regions'. He also learns to disregard public opinion, since the man 'who has attained to a life of reason' no longer needs to submit to the guidance of conventional mores. He has transcended them.[20] No longer distracted by the body or by the mob, the Cynic is free to focus on 'divine thoughts, which are stainless and pure'.[21] True followers of Diogenes will affirm with Plato the superiority of soul over body.[22] Whereupon the Roman Cynic steps 'outside himself' being assured 'the soul within him is divine'.[23] His soul is educated, in contrast to those who, by their ignorance, remain 'tied to the body' and popular opinion, against those who are by consequence 'subject to false opinion rather than truth'.[24] They are to be pitied, if not despised. In recuperating Cynicism then, Emperor Julian affords a complete reversal of the Cynic attitude.

*

Cynicism, of the 'sham' sort, was reproached for having no fixed *dogmata*. Surely a philosophy without central doctrine or code of belief is not a philosophy at all? In its more basic, un-recuperated and shambolic form, Cynicism remained unaccountable. Rather confusingly, Cynic philosophy operated without an 'end' or 'philosophical goal' otherwise known as its *telos*. This continues to baffle those who will not comprehend how one functions – philosophically speaking – in the absence of some goal or other. Consequently, even today's philosopher may insist that Cynicism was basically all about the pursuit of happiness, or virtue, or nature, or whatever.[25]

Educated Bodies

Cynics were not hostile to the notion one might wish to understand the world in which one lives. They were merely suspicious of the common prejudice that the world is best understood by adopting the conventions of rationality endorsed by a particular philosophical school. By rejecting intellectual culture, actively seeking destitution and hardship, the Cynic discovered the world through a series of practical confrontations with it.

*

The Cynics were great improvisers. What became their most famous tenets 'grew out of a continual process of ad hoc improvisation.' Against Plato's conception of the philosopher 'as a spectator of time and eternity', Diogenes was 'the philosopher of contingency, of life in the barrel'.[26] Diogenes did not seek out his barrel with the self-absorbed pathos of a martyr. According to one version of the story, upon arrival in Athens, Diogenes set up home in a storage jar simply because the little house he had hoped for could not be arranged in time.[27]

*

The philosopher of contingency lives without certainties and does not mourn their absence. The Cynic's life becomes an experiment. His philosophy constitutes 'a dialogue with the contingencies that shape the material conditions of existence'.[28] It takes the form of a rhetorical engagement, in the sense that the philosopher sends out provocations, examines the retorts provoked by them, and comes to understand the limits these retorts reflect. The challenge is to improvise a way of life that can sustain itself alongside and outside these limits.

*

Despite appearances, Cynics had nothing against the pursuit of virtue. Their contempt was merely heaped on the idea that virtue is best cultivated in a rarefied atmosphere.[29]

*

One portrait depicts the Cynic as a scout, sent 'in advance of humanity, to determine what may be favourable or hostile to man in the things of this world'. The Cynic learns to live without 'shelter, a home, or even a country' as he roams, running ahead of humanity, returning only to recount with fearless speech what he has discovered.[30] To speak fearlessly one becomes free of attachments, of duties that function as constraints.

*

The pursuit of a life without attachments had paradoxical effects. The Cynic began by stripping down existence, getting rid of anything that might be considered superfluous: Diogenes observes a boy drinking from his hollowed hand, then casts aside his wooden cup deciding it to be yet another unnecessary possession.[31] The Cynic of this more radical tradition was 'always looking for possible further destitution'. His was a 'dissatisfied poverty which strives to get back to the ground of the absolutely indispensable'. An 'indefinite poverty endlessly at work on itself'.[32] This deliberate impoverishment, committing the Cynic to a life of dirt and dishevelment, gave an independence of sorts, offering a kind of liberation from the trappings of wealth and civilized society. But it imposed a dependence of its own, since the Cynic became reliant on the alms of others. In the Greek and Roman context, with personal honour holding such high premium, this kind of dependence was almost unbearable. To court dishonour would be a radical test of one's resolve to live a different life. It would ensure the Cynic pursuit of poverty was more than a romantic affectation. The true Cynic actively seeks the shame of penury and hopes to survive it. For those who overcome the worst kinds of humiliation will have been purged of all false codes of conduct and notions of decency. The route to independence, rather oddly then, is through one's insufferable dependence on the charity of others. The Cynic must learn to be resolutely ungrateful when given alms, and be indifferent to those who cast judgement: One portrait depicts Demetrius, a first century Cynic from Corinth, refusing money from the Roman Emperor. "If he wanted to tempt me, he should have offered me the whole Empire".[33] This would be a real test of his mettle, of his determination to remain uncorrupted by power and wealth. The strength of his Cynicism, its indifference to things valued by his contemporaries, could only benefit from such refusal.

*

As an educational activity Cynicism is distinctly life affirming, in contrast to the stiff austerity of Platonism. For Plato, the body is an unfortunate appendage, filling us 'with loves and desires and fears and all sorts of fancies and a great deal of nonsense, with the result that we literally never get an opportunity to think at all about anything'. So long as we remain affected by it, 'there is no chance of our ever attaining satisfactorily to our object, which we assert to be Truth'.[34] For the Cynic, the body operates very differently. It becomes a site for the manifestation of truth. The body bears witness to reality, bringing us to question the existence of higher things. And so, whilst Plato sought to 'define the soul's being in its radical separation' from the life of the body, the Cynic operated in the opposite direction, seeking to reduce 'life to itself, to what it is in truth'. This basic truth was revealed through the very act of living as a Cynic, where 'all pointless conventions and all superfluous opinions' were cast aside, in a 'general stripping of existence' to its bare essentials…[35] In each case the 'true life' takes a different meaning. For Plato it is associated with the life that is simple, that does not conceal its intentions, the life that is straight and undeviating. It is completely at odds with the life of he who is 'prey to the multiplicity of his desires, appetites, and impulses of his soul'.[36] The true life is defined by its adherence to rules of good conduct (that Plato outlines), but more than this, by its overall unity. It is the life that remains unchanged in the face of adversity. It is lived by those few who maintain a secure and stable identity among corruption and upheaval. Ultimately, Plato assures us, the only souls passing judgement upon death will be the souls of those that have remained true in life…[37] For the Cynic, the 'true life' operates rather differently. It is the dog's life. Diogenes was known as the 'dog' and responded in kind: 'At a dinner some people were tossing bones to him as though he were a dog'. So Diogenes 'rid himself of them by pissing on them'.[38] Diogenes remained true to his philosophy, doing in public what others would conceal, acting without modesty or shame. He extended, if not radicalised, Plato's injunction to be unflagging in ones' commitment to truth and remain unchanged in the face of adversity. By acting the part of the dog Diogenes inverted the humiliation. He embraced his caricature, injuring the dignity of those pissed on.[39]

*

For the Greek philosopher, the 'true life' is a *sovereign life* in which the philosopher achieves, or at least works towards, self-mastery. This life deserves the epithet 'sovereign' since it describes a state of absolute self-control. No part of the philosopher's self thus imagined escapes the discipline and composure of a well-governed mind. This kind of self-possession is not only the high ideal to which Plato's philosopher king aspires. It is also the Roman Stoic dream of a figure such as Seneca. Crucially, it is believed that the sovereign life will be beneficial to others. Indeed the generosity of the sovereign life is constructed as if that were an obligatory component. The philosopher will provide students and friends alike with assistance and direction, extending the same care of self (a form of diligent self-denial) that resulted in the philosopher's self-mastery, to the care of the student or friend. There will be wider benefits too, since the philosopher's life offers a lesson that is of greater, if not universal significance. The splendour and brilliance of the sovereign life, the life of complete self-mastery, 'adorns humankind'[40] and educates it too, having an influence so profoundly far reaching it continues long after the philosopher's exemplary life has ended... The Cynic also claims to be living a sovereign existence, to be a king amongst men, except this philosopher has achieved self-composure rather differently, and with regard to external temptations and humiliations. The Cynic chooses to pursue destitution, 'pushing back the limits of what he can bear',[41] in order to develop a completely different way of relating to the world. This sovereign life still has a duty to others, a duty of care. Yet the Cynic's generosity takes the form of a personal sacrifice and a public scandal designed to confront those it upsets with their afflictions. The Cynic life involves a dedication to others that operates without gratitude or recognition. The Cynic does not offer a beautiful example for others to emulate. The Cynic life does not adorn humankind, it besmirches it. The Cynic still adopts the role of public benefactor, but Cynic generosity is self-consciously and deliberately harsh. As Diogenes used to say: "Other dogs bite their enemies, but I my friends, so as to save them".[42]

*

One might describe the Cynic as an 'aggressive benefactor'.[43] Yet this would downplay the benign violence of other breeds of benefaction. It would imply theirs is a generosity without aggression. The philosopher who gives kindly advice, who perhaps 'adorns' humankind with the beautiful example of his presence, is also aggressive in promoting his version of the good. The Cynic is only unique for openly declaring his aggressive intent. As an educational project, Cynicism embraces quite explicitly 'the form of a battle'.[44] For Platonists and Stoics, the battle is covered over with refinement, taking form as a philosopher's fight against his passions, desires and false appetites, as he hopes to ensure 'the victory of reason over his own appetites or his soul over his body'.[45] Some version of the philosopher's fight, along with its recommended destination, is then prescribed for others. The Cynics also battled with passions and appetites, yet this battle was extended to 'customs, conventions, institutions, laws, and a whole condition of humanity' that our passions and appetites are symptomatic of.[46] Hence the Cynic battle is 'an explicit, intentional, and constant aggression directed at humanity in general'.[47] The Cynic sought to release humanity from its current attachments so that it might work towards another life, and another world. In this context, the truths offered by the Cynic grow in strength and quality to the extent they scandalise, bringing unthinking commitments to the surface, rendering them visible and hence open to adjustment. By contrast, the 'true life' of the conventional philosopher, which carries to perfection the virtues and qualities that are only said to be weakly expressed in ordinary lives, comes across as distinctly conservative, if not reactionary. By rejecting accepted values in an attempt to transform them, the Cynic's was a thankless task. The more thankless the better.

*

Diogenes could have left Athens and lived as a hermit of sorts. If his was a simple regression to the animalistic, it might have been pursued anywhere. But Diogenes remained in Athens participating in a cultural transformation the destination of which remained uncertain. Diogenes did not teach: 'Be like an animal'. Rather, he taught; 'Bear witness to the animal and the possibility that anything which exceeds this animal form may be superfluous, and is certainly contingent'.

*

Whilst Socrates famously received word from the Delphic oracle, Diogenes had his own encounter. Or at least, Diogenes forges one with a 'counterfeit oracle' of his own. His encounter was 'a rascal's take on the dignity of oracles', a parody of Socrates' own.[48] Diogenes, so the story goes, was instructed to 'change the value of the currency' in the phrase: *parakharattein to nomisma*. The word *nomisma* has multiple significations, referring to legal tender, but also norms, customs, and laws.[49] Inciting subversive if not criminal activity, became a defining idea in the life of the Cynic. It was taken to refer to the position a Cynic must take with relation to any social convention in circulation. The command to change the value of the currency is nevertheless ambiguous: A currency can simply be devalued, by defacing a coin, so it no longer can be used in exchange for goods. Or, one might start with a coin that carries a certain effigy (such as the reigning monarch), erase that effigy and replace it with a different one (depicting accumulated wealth and exploitation). This would 'enable the coin to circulate with its true value' since it is now stamped 'with another, better, and more adequate effigy'.[50] Here the Cynic endeavours to show that the lives of others are 'no more than counterfeit'.[51] By changing the value of the currency, coins that once had value become worthless, and things once considered worthless, gain value. The life of the Cynic embodies this switch by putting its conception of 'the true currency with its true value into circulation'.[52] This life breaks with existing systems of value. By making a spectacle of itself, it demonstrates another life is possible (another currency could be minted). The 'true life' becomes that life which is radically opposed to its surroundings. It exposes those surroundings in all their constraint, whilst speaking of the possible existence of another radically different conception of the truth. Unlike the Platonic conception of another transcendent world (the world of the Forms) which is used to denigrate this world and tie it to a death-bound education of the soul; the Cynic conception of another life is used to denigrate this life in a way that invigorates it and causes it to explode its confines.

*

If the soul is to be educated, it must be convinced that somewhere, somehow its activities and inclinations are visible. For a Stoic philosopher such as Epictetus it was sufficient to argue God dwells within us. Hence all impure thoughts and dirty actions sully him as much as they do us.[53] Consequently one lives in private as if nothing remains concealed, developing inhibitions and restraints. But the Cynic decides to radicalise the idea that nothing is concealed, by acting it out. The Cynic responds to the injunction, the true life is the life that has nothing to hide, by hiding nothing. The Cynic does everything in the open, having no home or private place to retreat to. This removes the constraining influence of a conscience that is designed precisely for those private spaces which must be convinced of their culpability. Since these private spaces have become the residence of the conscience, this 'staging of life in its material and everyday reality under the real gaze of others, of everyone else, or at any rate of the greatest possible number of others',[54] renders the moral order imposed by the conscience ineffective.

*

Cynic teaching, when not directly exemplified through the life of a Cynic philosopher, was conveyed through brief anecdotes, recollected gestures and retorts, ironic encounters and witty remarks. These were designed to be 'as portable and memorable as jokes'.[55] Hence they were passed on by means sharply contrasted to those of more traditional philosophical doctrines. In Foucault's words, once more; traditional philosophy consists in 'reactualizing a forgotten and misunderstood core of thought in order to make it the point of departure and source of authority' of a more recent tradition.[56] It was a matter of defining oneself in relation to what Aristotle or

Plato had originally said, for instance.[57] By contrast, Cynics had a very different relationship to their predecessors. Episodes from the lives of past Cynics were recalled not because these episodes and their doctrinal content had been forgotten (indeed it mattered little if the episodes recounted were actual occurrences or mythical constructs). Rather, they were recalled because today's philosopher might no longer be 'equal to these examples' due to some sort of decline, enfeeblement or decadence that has bled our capacity for Cynicism.[58] Past Cynics were remembered to provoke present actors to reconsider their conduct, and perhaps enable 'the strength of conduct' exemplified in the actions of past Cynics 'to be restored' to those lacking courage.[59]

*

The educational legacy of Cynicism remains obscure. It is less directly accessible as a history than the educational legacies of the more formally endowed philosophical schools. These latter histories can be traced through institutional chronicles and the descent of canonical texts. They were teaching institutions in the traditional sense, with the potential to multiply their activities with missionary zeal. But the Cynic accumulated disciples if at all only by accident. This was the education of a life of provocations, always foreclosed by death. The educational descent of Cynicism is episodic and erratic. The history of Cynicism is complicated too by its gradual transformation from a term referring to an ascetic way of life, to a term (with a small 'c') used to describe a more generalised sense of disenchantment. The Cynics criticised the culture in which they found themselves contrasting it to nature as expressed by the animality of each Cynic. By asserting oneself as an animal and reducing life to its bare essentials, the Cynic implicitly questioned the intrinsic worth of refined customs and cultured attitudes that surround civilized beings. The Cynic way of life was designed to scandalise contemporaries, draw out their prejudices and bear witness to the possibility of a completely different attitude to existence.[60] More recent cynicism still casts a suspicious gaze on cultured refinements and rarefied customs, yet its scandalising impulse operates without direction. It operates without the Cynic's pursuit of animality. No longer convinced of the point of bodily engagement, no longer offering an alternative way of life grounded in an encounter with nature, or in an encounter with what culture rejects, this cynicism is overcome by apathy.

*

Cynicism has other descendants. The wandering Christian monk was also a 'martyr of the truth',[61] bearing witness to this truth by way of contrast between the freely chosen destitution of the ascetic life, and the life of those still enjoying a materially well off but spiritually hollow existence. Here Foucault offers a tentative foray into the 'long history of Christian Cynicism',[62] suggesting it preserved and passed on many of the 'themes, attitudes, and forms of behaviour' observable in the Cynics to the spiritual movements of medieval Europe.[63] It was, he suggests, a 'particularly lively, intense, and strong practice in all the efforts at reform which were opposed to the Church, its institutions, its increasing wealth, and its moral laxity'.[64] This Christian Cynicism was designed to force ecclesiastical institutions in all their splendour and corruption to face some basic Christian truths, expressed in the wretched bodily piety of the medieval ascetic. Yet this was a very different kind of ascetic practice. Whereas the Cynic acted on this life to bring it to the point where it passes over into another form of worldly existence, Christian asceticism incorporated Platonic elements, invoking a contrast between this worldly life and the true life of the Christian hereafter.[65] Its ultimate objectives were externally ordained and pre-defined. Similarly constrained, the Christian martyr also adapted Cynic technique, inviting the wrath of a social order that was scandalized by the martyr's determined obedience to another, higher authority. Martyrdom became the ultimate embodiment of one's commitment to a truth fundamentally at odds with one's surroundings. The daring insolence of the martyr nevertheless expressed a diluted version of Cynic courage. The martyr desired not simply to inspire others, but to exhibit him or herself before a watchful God, hoping such displays of trust would bring salvation. The Cynic, by contrast, had no such contract or guarantee. One could argue, as does Foucault, that revolutionary movements later inherited some of the attitudes and forms of behaviour variously passed on by Christian martyrs and ascetics. In a similar way they would incorporate a higher authority, or telos into their practice, which becomes their driving rationale. They would also remain marginal to those great organisational efforts that sought to define and impose a revolutionary discipline and a temporary set of values on their combatants and members. These marginal attitudes would be expressed through the figure of the 'militant' with little time for party discipline. The militant would have the boldness to embody a form of existence that already broke with the social, political and economic conventions that were to be overthrown. This life would not restrain its impulses for the purposes of future victory. The uncompromising militant would shamelessly scandalise sympathetic reformists and unsympathetic reactionaries with equal zeal and pleasure.

A Returned Diogenes
Cynicism drops to cynicism with a lower case 'c', once

taken up by that modern figure, the rebel without a cause. With no truth to bear witness too, and faced with a question: 'How to live if nothing is true'?[66]

*

Committed nihilists are rare. Against affirmation, mass cynicism makes for a distinctly non-committal nihilism, a decidedly weak nihilistic impulse. Today's nihilist tends to be sickly, removed and bad tempered.

*

The committed nihilist does not think in order to revolt, but revolts in an attempt to think. In an educational context, the committed nihilist follows through with the suspicion modern education lacks value, seriously broaching a predicament where the values promoted by modern education have become institutional affects. Drawing from a long tradition of Cynic engagement, this figure *acts out* his or her educational reservations. The most expensively educated nihilists in particular (those occupying lucrative university positions) focus resolutely on that Nietzschean adage: *'Success has always been the biggest liar'* as if it were their closest mantra.[67] Our most educated nihilists would not simply feel embarrassed by their education and by the conceit of their educated class (for those merely embarrassed can still enjoy the pleasures of false modesty). They *act upon* their conviction that education lacks value by seeking to unsettle and render precarious the high status and privilege still conferred upon them by their educational attainments. And yet, the Cynical educator, that practitioner of educated nihilism, remains within the confines of education as Diogenes remained in Athens. This educator will not depart easily or willingly.

*

The educated nihilist offends us. By definition, this creature only rejects education after enjoying its benefits. An odious situation, though claims were never made here for its moral decency. The educated nihilist is indecent by profession.

*

Shitting in public no longer vitiates society. Other famous acts of Cynic shamelessness would be similarly ineffective. All such perversions have since been subsumed by psychologies that presume to treat them. They have been adopted by disciplines that take these perversions for their bread and butter. There is even a 'Diogenes' syndrome' for homeless people exhibiting signs of extreme self-neglect. [68] In our late modern context, acts of bodily shamelessness designed to call into question the very values that animate the scandalised, only fuel the system. Shameless acts reinforce those very disciplines that seek to normalise behaviour by constructing abnormalities as sufficient reason for remedial action. Undeniably this is a relief (in a different sense) for today's educated Cynic, who must look elsewhere for inspiration. But the relief is short-lived. The Cynic's task has become far more punishing.

*

We can imagine along with Sloterdijk a *'returned Diogenes'* climbing out of his Athenian tub, into recent history. [69] He gets caught up in two world wars and numerous other conflagrations, genocides and massacres. He strolls through the principal sites of capitalism and communism watching the former expand through a series of aggressive cycles and the latter undergo the most brutal implosions. He eventually stumbles forth into the political apathy of our present that no longer dreams of changing its conditions of existence. He witnesses how our most progressive contemporaries confront their own century of ecological and social catastrophe by purchasing ethical beans and aspiring to pious reservations of 'carbon neutrality' as they, and we, befoul the rest of the planet. And in the midst of this cynical disorder Diogenes finally encounters education, and is surprised to hear a repeated promise, that through education 'all can achieve success'. Whilst Diogenes had taught: 'Be ready for anything', what he now sees goes beyond comprehension.[70] Though Diogenes had a pretty low opinion of his fellow Athenians, what he finds in our present (a present in many respects already thoroughly perverted) seems to have descended so far into absurdity that it is beneath subversion. Diogenes is rightly fearful of our psychiatric institutions and so comes across a little muted. Yet his silence is more enduring. A productive response to our present impasse, a real game changer as they say, seems at first beyond him.

*

The *modus operandi* of the Cynic – 'living differently' – must face its inevitable adoption by capital. Here May 1968 serves as a galling reminder of how attempts to reinvent daily life can be outmanoeuvred. They were cut short by a revolution in the workplace, so the argument goes, one that increasingly valued autonomy, inspiration and the odd wacky idea, rather than conformity and protocol.[71] Everyday existence is now relentlessly exploited to breathe life back into the dead hand of capital.[72] Workers and educational subjects are expected to take upon themselves a stylization of life that will render them permanently adaptable to the whims of the marketplace. Hence those who approach Nietzsche with fresh ears today, hearing how he flirted with the idea of an

Übermensch – the heroic few who, having achieved authentic existence through self-assertion, free themselves from Christian morality – will fear not the seeds of some Nazi ideology. They come to see a version of this quest is all too common now. Feverishly promoted by capital: To Be Yourself, to the exclusion of all others, authentic to the point of nothing, to the point of destruction in the face of such impossible responsibilities, is the modern ultimatum.[73] Individual lives are framed increasingly in this way; folded back on themselves, as lives of 'self-stylization *vis-à-vis* the cultivation of [potentially counter-]cultural taste, body image and so forth'.[74] Our bodies, our tastes and inclinations, have become objects of training, therapy, adornment and 'free' expression. These bodies exist as cultural and counter-cultural projects, requiring continual inspection, adjustment and readjustment. Our lives have been invested with a quest for enrichment, alteration, for new experiences, new trends. And so, should today's Cynic manage to avoid pathologization or arrest for indecency, the embodied practices this Cynic displays would be perceived as just another lifestyle choice – albeit with exhibitionist tendencies – operating within the boundaries of liberal acceptability.

*

Refusing those selves, confronting these self-governing agents of power, inevitably calls for a more radical act. It leads those resisting to new forms of self-repudiation. In the Cynic tradition at its most extreme, this entails a form of bodily and subjective rejection akin to suicide. For such a refusal of self would, by definition, go against our very nature as it has been constituted by power. We are agents of power, we do its bidding, we produce its effects, we adapt it to circumstance. By living we fulfil its urges. In this context, self-repudiation would be an act of refusal, of revolt, of a kind Diogenes attempted. This old dog, so the story goes, finally expired by holding his breath.[75] The point of interest is the impossibility of the act. Who commits suicide by holding their breath? Nobody. The very notion is absurd. But with a returned Cynic, suicide rises up the philosophical agenda. It could even become the 'only truly philosophical problem', as Camus once put it.[76] The Cynic approaches suicide without appeal to external forces, without relying on chemistry, or gravity, or whatever. The Cynic refuses all assistance that might entail capitulation to power, a 'giving up' in the face of insuperable odds, a laying down before that which cannot be defeated. The Cynic repudiates the 'authentic' self of self-government, refusing that mythical but affective self in an act of defiance that produces the Cynic. Cynic refusal does not entail a practice of the self that folds back on itself, giving another spin on the injunction to be yourself. Rather Cynic refusal folds outwards.

*

For the educated nihilist, career suicide might be reconceptualised as a form of impossible suicide, akin to holding one's breath. It would be a project where one affirms the inevitable end of one's career, committing to the practice of career suicide all one's working life. This would go against the very nature of the educator as he or she has been constructed. It would dig away at her core attachment to education without which, she believes, she could not operate. Crucially, the pursuit of career suicide would match in its pitch the progress of one's career, where it is all the more intensely pursued as one's position in the organisation becomes more secure. According to this hierarchy of transgressions, the university vice chancellor would be the biggest educational heretic in town.

*

Do not misunderstand the invitation. The outer limits of acceptable conduct are sufficiently clear. But how is the educator otherwise constrained excepting obvious taboos? That such and such would be tantamount to 'career suicide' is a common enough refrain in work settings. Less exaggerated expressions of the same sentiment would be, that such and such risks too much; that it is not worth it; that there will be comeback; that one would be endangering one's position, and so on. In the university this fear is sometimes nurtured by a threat in the small print: a contract may not be issued, or if issued may not be renewed, or if permanent the employee may be fired for bringing the corporation 'into disrepute'. Or less obviously, positions are slowly made untenable, with reprisals obscuring themselves through a time delay. Fortunately for academics (and unfortunately for the pursuit of truth), they have become increasingly adept at the necessary self-chastisements and pre-emptive self-discipline that will keep them far from trouble. Most successful careerists curtail their infractions so diligently that each breach of convention manages to fall short of that lower, hazy border which defines the onset of risky behaviour. Most often, indeed, we barely notice when our colleagues rebel, even though they themselves may be experiencing all the stress and excitement of a transgressive act. But in noting such timorous traits I do not ridicule today's educator. I merely recognise that for this figure, bravery is manifested in the pettiest misdeeds. To encourage these timid souls (of which I am one) to approach the boundaries of their educated existence, is not to suggest they work towards a militant individualism. To push one's cynicism to its capitalisation is not to cut oneself off from others in solitary protest. Rather, the plight of the educated Cynic is similar to that of the beggar Cynic. The irony of the latter is that in pursuing independence, in cutting oneself off from all luxuries and commitments yet remaining in Athens, the beggar Cynic becomes only more dependent. In seeking independence from all cultural mores, the beggar Cynic comes to rely upon the charity of the system he subverts. But the Cynic overcomes this double bind, refusing to display any gratitude when alms are given. Even better, the Cynic *insults* those who give alms. The indifference of the beggar Cynic is designed to undermine this relationship of charity, where those who give alms would normally use their connection with the beggar to affirm themselves as benefactors. In a similar way the educated Cynic refuses all compassion or well-intended advice. This calms the situation, mollifies the Cynic, but most importantly, it allows one's compatriots to return to work. Against this, the purpose of Cynicism in the workplace is to make the discomfort involved a shared and productive experience, as we attempt to overcome or at least bring into question this thing we call education.[77]

*

Paulo Freire once called upon critical pedagogues to commit 'class suicide'.[78] His counsel was this: In order to side with the exploited and dispossessed, the critical pedagogue must finally, and conclusively, close the door on his or her bourgeois existence. In his *Letters to Guinea-Bissau* (extending an argument made by guerrilla leader Amilcar Cabral[79]), Freire recognises that such a 'death' will not be 'easily accepted even by those verbally committed to a revolutionary stance'.[80] Though intellectuals may agree in principle that the new society might require a 'different conception of education'[81] they will not be able imagine a conception of education so different that it has no place for them and their kind in it. In a similar way, the educated nihilist also struggles to imagine a conception of education so different that his or her 'educated' credentials become questionable appendages. And yet, whilst most educated critics of the Freirean tradition would understand the logic of this invitation to commit class suicide but would characteristically fail to take it up,[82] the educated nihilist also finds the invitation to be incoherent. After all, class suicide is recommended so as to foster a more authentic educational encounter, precisely the thing the educated nihilist has given up on. Militant action for the latter represents something very different, that is, an attempt to live without education, or at least entertain in its presence the most radical form of doubt.

*

For the educated nihilist, career suicide is approached as a 'limit-experience'. It is pursued as an ongoing series of encounters with the limits imposed by one's place of work. Discomfort is necessary. Since these limits are already absorbed within the subject who seeks to confront them, because they are deeply formative of the professional self, each confrontation is experienced as pain. But the educated Cynic pursues each 'limit-experience that wrenches the subject from itself' with abject determination. The Cynic sees to it that the subject of education – the educator within each educated person – 'is no longer itself, or that it is brought to its annihilation or its dissolution'.[83]

*

A direct, unmediated encounter with failure, would finish the educator off. A conception of mastery still haunts the profession, and sustains it. Admittedly the pursuit of mastery has been reduced of late, from the aspiration to a high and distant ideal, to a more straightforward estimation of one's ability to meet desired outputs.

Academics in particular are governed like this; they govern one another and themselves like that. As a peer network they collude in judging one another's outputs, servicing the machine that turns intellectual work into measurable commodities. For academics, then, the opening gambit in their revolt could simply be an interruption of efforts to satisfy other academics, in particular the peer reviewer, that benchmark of quality and conformity. The revolting academic might cease production altogether, failing to churn out the required bids and papers, or, better still, would write in a style that lacks due seriousness. A remarkably difficult effect to sustain:

> PLAYBOY: In some of your books – especially The Sirens of Titan and Slaughterhouse-Five – there's a serious notion that all moments in time exist simultaneously... VONNEGUT: You understand, of course, that everything I say is horseshit. PLAYBOY: Of course. VONNEGUT: Well, we do live our lives simultaneously. That's a fact... PLAYBOY: It still seems paradoxical. VONNEGUT: That is because what I just said to you is horseshit.'[84]

Lacking seriousness, the revolting academic ensures work cannot be traded for points, since in academic terms such outputs are unacceptable currency. In response to the well-known refrain, 'publish or perish', this academic would rather perish outright, or at least publish perished works – works considered too far gone by one's peers. From this position, each time the academic is drawn back to institutional productivity, each time a paper is submitted, and then accepted, there will be a little pang, a sensation of failure.

*

But Cynicism still seems beyond our grasp. The pursuit of success and mastery is so endemic to education that even failure is recast as its opposite. When educators leave their profession, they risk affirming education in a parting shot. Each departure testifies to the individual who was too authentic, too true to education to tolerate what it has become. Even those claiming to leave education cannot show it contempt.

VII

SPIRIT OF HEAVINESS

Held in denial
Forever held in denial, mastery of an aborted, duplicitous kind catches and keeps us mid-gasp. With a promise of mastery, education claimed to elevate, even make the philosopher immune to the world below and its persecutions. Yet mastery was yoked to its opposite: the enslavement of philosopher to philosophical doctrine, for mastery also required discipline and self-control. It attached the self to an ordinance that promised sovereignty but demanded obedience. With Christianity, self-mastery became 'an instrument of subordination' of more complete effect, as spiritual training occupied the entire life of the Christian subject.[1] It committed its practitioners to a regime of power that would take care of their entire life in all its detail and for the rest of its duration.[2] At the same time, the promise of transcendence became ever more spectral, dependent on

God's will. The strength of will exhibited by the self-denying Christian was of secondary importance, for at the gates of heaven, God decides. On earth, the Christian monk is warned against pursuing any self-denying ordinance to excess. And so we find Cassian denouncing those who would cast themselves down wells, fast excessively, or cross deserts without food in an effort to demonstrate just how catastrophically they had achieved self-mastery, purging themselves of natural inclinations and desires.[3] These were not acts of extreme piety. They were symptomatic of pride. And pride is of the devil.

*

Mastery holds within itself the danger of its fulfilment, a danger that theological orders and educational regimes are concerned to mitigate. In the first centuries after Christ, with extreme asceticism on the rise, the old but sinuous link connecting the promise of mastery to the necessity of enslavement calcified, and then broke. In perfecting their self-denials, early Christian ascetics (those Cassian warned against) became increasingly indifferent to pain and discomfort, and thereby removed themselves beyond the grasp of power. Ascetics denied themselves so completely that little remained for power to gain purchase on. This posed a challenge to organised Christianity, since its most potent ascetics had effectively reversed the self-denials of monastic obedience, transforming these denials into a form of 'egoistic self-mastery'.[4] Monastic and ecclesiastical institutions were faced with the task of bringing self-mastery back within their control. They would purge themselves of all vagrant, self-sufficient, ascetic heresies, reclaiming all marvels and self-flagellations as their own. Eventually self-mastery of this more duplicitous kind would, like pastoral care, slip its 'doctrinal moorings' and migrate to a secular context.[5] Education remains in awe of mastery but preaches denial.

Education yokes its members to the pursuit of mastery but will not allow that mastery to become realised as such. Mastery haunts education as its most enduring, unrealisable promise.

*

What education promises mastery of changes: From ancient self in pursuit of wisdom, to medieval body desiring knowledge of God, to modern subject of autonomous reason, until finally, we arrive at the promise we might master our own performativities. By definition mastery is to remain spectral. Our nihilism is the product of this framework, this belief that education requires higher objectives, a belief so entrenched that as each objective comes under attack another is substituted, or when substitutes are left wanting, we are launched into overproduction. For we scarcely know how to operate let alone educate without the promise of mastery. Nihilism is an unavoidable affliction. It has us in its grasp. Those claiming to exist beyond its reach are in denial. There is no quick and easy escape. We are trapped in the digestive tract of Western history. Attached to a promise never delivered, we are produced as disappointments. Masters of everything and nothing.

Sade as Educator

Education is opposed to nihilism, as hope is opposed to despair. One is the assumed antidote for the other. Yet those hoping to escape nihilism *through education* rather than in spite of it will find themselves poisoned by false remedies. Nihilism is not escaped by perpetuating what produced it. Education cannot solve nihilism, it only colludes with it. Of course, as educators and educated people we remain unmoved by such claims. We are forever attached to our poisons: Surely the fight against nihilism is best fought as a fight for education, as a battle for the realisation of an educational project finally made good, a form of education that gives up this ancient game of deferral, deceit and perpetual disappointment, and in full sincerity finally delivers what it promises? Since we remain unmoved, let us take our poison instead, and judge its effects. To those educators who remain wedded, despite everything, to the idea of education, itself dominated by the idea of mastery – and this represents most of us – it is worth experiencing how an exit might look, one that gives mastery a chance to express itself without doubling back and denying its realisation. This would be an exercise in *Sade's Reason*, as Maurice Blanchot described it. For there is no better example of mastery run amok than is found in the writing of that eighteenth century libertine, the Marquis de Sade. We find here an attempt to practice mastery without duplicity, without the accompanying call to self-denial. We encounter education as mastery, as its fulfilment.

*

Justine; Juliette; Philosophy of the Boudoir; The 120 Days of Sodom: scandalous books that scandalise us still. And yet, whilst there is 'no better symbol of scandal' than the Marquis de Sade, 'the scandalous audacity of his thought has remained long unknown'.[6] This was Blanchot's analysis. Sade's books were excessive in every sense, that much we perceive. What we fail to see is how, in their excess, they exaggerate our own basic attachments. We find ourselves confronted with works of horrific, 'unsurpassable monstrosity', though 'rationalist in construction' and 'pedagogic in genre'.[7] Sade's offence, in short, was to follow through. It was to express the idea of mastery inherent in reason, and the idea of education inherent in mastery. It was to bring education, mastery and reason to their conclusion.

*

Sade's texts are instructional, educational.[8] They are relentlessly, tediously educational, perhaps unrivalled in their singular commitment to instruction. Juliette, their most accomplished student, must surpass, then abandon, perhaps even sacrifice each teacher she encounters in her pursuit of mastery.[9] Initially Juliette misunderstands, hoping that her teacher will be her protector in crime and debauchery. But as Noirceuil explains, "one must learn to manage by oneself, to rely upon one's own solitary resources".[10] Juliette must learn to practice mastery alone, eventually becoming master of herself. Her education demands absolute commitment to vice. Failure is inexcusable. Even the slightest indication of failure will invoke severe reprisal, if not an attempt on her life from those who were formerly her teachers.[11] Only later does she realize that, by extension, her "whole ambition shall be someday to surpass my teacher"...[12] One might expect that in attempting to surpass her teachers in mastery Juliette would aspire to become the most exemplary teacher herself. Indeed, this is what Juliette first assumes:

> I keenly sense my need of instruction, I no less keenly desire to educate someone: I must have a teacher, yes, and I must have a pupil too.[13]

Yet by the time Juliette finally acquires her pupil, she is on the road to becoming such an accomplished libertine, so apathetic to the plight of others that she loses all interest in teaching those far beneath her.[14] Juliette so bores of her assigned pupil Alexandrine that she dispatches of her, and her biography, in a mere paragraph so as to avoid ever having to mention her again.[15] Rather significantly, Alexandrine's swift demise is attributed to the very poor instruction she received from her tutor, Juliette.[16] Hence, in Sade we discover how the desire to outdo one's teachers in mastery could be fatal to teaching, and so to education. The desire to achieve full blown mastery certainly does not breed a desire to surpass one's teachers in teaching, to become a better teacher.

*

If Juliette's teachers are ever annihilated, this occurs only if they are found wanting from the perspective of her own developing supremacy. She respects her teachers as long as their libertine mastery is assured. They are heeded for as long as they can teach, and teach by example. Otherwise Juliette would have "bled them white", as she puts it, at the first opportunity.[17] Overcome here, then, are centuries of Christian toleration, where mastery is to be diligently pursued but never presumed to become fully manifest, even in the most holy, for that would lead to a dangerous asceticism. Overcoming all tolerations, the libertine student no longer suffers the teacher who does not bear out, in all completeness, his philosophical teachings in his actions. Through education, the libertine adopts that ancient logic of mastery found inherent in education, unshackles it, and drives the pursuit of mastery to its hilt.

*

Libertine mastery has its subtleties. In the context of Sade's writing we might associate it with and perhaps reduce it to a form of phallic supremacy. Or we might find ourselves reminded of Greek pederasty in its aboriginal relationship to philosophy (so many of Sade's victims are children), where, in one reading, we observe how over and again 'a greater man penetrates a lesser man with his knowledge'. This, after all, is a classic paradigm in Western pedagogy.[18] Such conclusions are too easy, however. Though Sade's texts are all about penetration, the penetrating agent is not singular in its form, nor is it always modeled on the phallus. The libertine often 'socratizes' (as he calls it) by other means, and does so not merely for pleasure, or to dominate, but for purposes of examination in both a medical and educational sense. The libertine will enter the body by any means, cutting into it if necessary. In so doing, the better libertine, like the better educator, does not simply 'put in'; he also 'leads out' from what is found there.[19] His mastery depends upon a prior investigation into the internal consistency of Man, of what makes him tick, of how his juices flow, of how he errs. He renders Man entirely material. He destroys the conceit of Man by making Man the object of type of study, a vivisection, which leads to the most intimate and base observations. His investigation is at once an enquiry into what we are in body and of what must be overcome.[20] Hence mastery of this kind is less assured, and more intricated in the problems of an 'irrational bodily materiality' than we might otherwise assume.[21] With Sade, mastery eventually confronts the impossibility of its realization. It destroys itself in the attempt.

*

The libertine's self-mastery reaches towards complete egoism, complete in the sense that the libertine remains unaffected by his crimes. Self-possessed, deracinated, his ego can indulge itself without consideration. His crimes obey no external logic or internal demand; they are an expression of the libertine's own prolific creativity. Becoming inaccessible to others, the libertine asserts his or her will without appeal ("the most enjoyable crimes are the motiveless ones. The victim must be perfectly innocent: if we have sustained some harm from him it legitimates the harm we do him"[22]). In this sense his mastery is complete; the libertine wilfully destroys others, even destroys himself for no other reason. But this exalted state is only achieved at great expense, by defeating Man, God, and even Nature (though not necessarily in that order[23]). The libertine must overcome each framework of appeal through force of will alone, exaggerating each metaphysical attachment to the point of its own annulment. Through the pursuit of mastery, even mastery itself must eventually expire.

*

In Blanchot's view, Sade remains a 'prodigious enigma' so long as we fail to interrogate the logic exemplified in his work. [24] Perhaps last of all will we permit a confrontation between Sade and education, for Sade threatens education as he threatens reason, not by stepping outside its boundaries, but by exaggerating its own inherently debauched tendencies to dramatic effect.[25]

*

With Sade we find depicted 'sovereign man', inaccessible because nothing can hurt him. He dominates others and tortures them with such delight in order to experience just how dispassionate he has become. What is murder to him? Nothing but "a little organized matter disorganized; a few compositional changes, the combination of some molecules disturbed and broken...tossed back into the crucible of nature".[26] As Juliette's first teacher explains, he will "execute every atrocity, great and small, with a constant and inviolable serenity".[27] He knows 'how to turn all distaste into tastes, all repugnance into attractions'. He 'sets about accomplishing the enormous task of completely enumerating every anomaly, every distraction, every human possibility. He must experience everything in order to be at the mercy of nothing'.[28] The libertine even welcomes the gallows with pleasure.[29] 'Against such a Power, what can the law do? It intends to punish such a man, but it rewards him, and it thrills him by demeaning him.'[30] He is sovereign for that reason. But he is sovereign too in the more complete sense that each time he sacrifices a victim, he decides 'to sacrifice a thousand more'. He is not tied to his victim in a relation of dependence. He does not derive meaning from the individual he annihilates; his victim barely exists as a distinct sentient being. Each victim is 'but a simple component, indefinitely exchangeable, within an enormous erotic equation'.[31]

*

Mastery of such monstrous proportions is not achieved without considerable effort. The libertine becomes sovereign only after passing through all prior stages of debauchery. In the less practised libertine we discover someone who derives pleasure from aggravating the plight of others. His is a "pleasure of comparison"[32] – where the suffering of others only brings out, by way of contrast, his own happiness. His mastery is dependent on the subjugation of others, a relationship that brings into question his own strength. For 'by comparing his situation with that of the wretched, the fortunate man ineluctably identifies himself with the wretched one'. At this intermediate stage, the mind of the libertine 'remains riveted on the reality of the other, which it seeks to deny... The debauchee remains attached to the victim of his lusts'. He is obsessed with his victim's suffering, and this is his weakness. This debauchee has not yet achieved sovereignty. His pride and his sense of self-worth is dependent on the defeat of others. But the sovereign man 'does not attach himself to any object; caught up in the perpetual motion of nature, he obeys his impulses and looks upon nature's creatures as no more than its foam'.[33]

*

Sovereign man may have succeeded in detaching himself from the pleasure of comparison, yet the pursuit of mastery has him enslaved to a destructive, ultimately self-destructive path of voluptuous annihilation. Like the extreme ascetic so feared by Cassian, the soul that wishes to become free must first deny all pleasure, removing every last temptation. Unlike the ascetic, the libertine does so by pursuing all temptation, destroying all pleasures, and in so doing destroys everything else besides. Hence Sade's writings are 'littered with the corpses of libertines, struck down at the height of their glory'.[34] Sovereign man may achieve mastery, but he does so by annihilating all things, including himself. By reducing all he touches to nothing, the most practised libertine 'only makes this nothingness manifest'. The world in which he lives 'is a desert; the beings he encounters there are less than things, less than shadows. While studying them, tormenting them and destroying them, he does not seize upon their life, but verifies their nothingness. He becomes master of their nonexistence, and he draws great pleasure from this'.[35] Quite literally the libertine realises his nihilism. He follows through with that tradition in Western metaphysics which associates being with a higher realm. He gives expression to a tradition which denigrates this world below by associating it with a process of transient becoming. This world is nothing by comparison to the world above, a prejudice Sade takes great pleasure in exploiting. Sade pursues that 'disavowal of reality' upon which 'the language of the West' was built,[36] by treating its members as they conceptualise themselves, by approaching them as if they were 'already dead', as if they were already worth nothing.[37]

*

In Sade's world those seeking mastery achieve it through an enormous, monstrous negation. Blanchot again: 'This negation, which is carried out on a massive scale, which no individual instance is enough to satisfy, is essentially destined to surpass the plane of human existence.'[38] It requires a kind of boldness no philosopher has managed hitherto. Sadean man frees himself in relation to his victim because he wishes to exist independently. He wishes to become the perfect philosopher by virtue of his separation from worldly things. Admittedly, he does so by engaging in bodily acts, but he is never consumed by the act. For all his commitment to bodily perversion he remains a philosopher. As Simone de Beauvoir once put it, sovereign man never 'loses himself in his animal nature'. His exploits are so premeditated and cerebral that 'philosophic discourse, far from dampening his ardor, acts as an aphrodisiac'.[39] He is no Cynic, then. With Sade we find the wildest hope of philosophy realised; 'a lucid mind inhabits a body which is being degraded into matter'.[40] But Sadean man does not stop there. He reduces God to nothing also, and thereby reveals not only the monstrous negation upon which Western philosophy is built. He reveals what Nietzsche describes as the 'empty fiction'[41] that justified such negation. For the world was denied in the name of otherworldly beings and ideas, in the name of spectres that finally coalesced, with Christianity, in the figure of God. With Christianity, knowledge of God and access to heaven became dependent on practices of Christian self-denial. And yet, as Sade portrays it, this monstrous order of discourse will itself eventually crumble, for nihilism entails the 'death of God' too, in a final painful, drawn-out negation.[42] Again in Sade's hands this death is too much even for today's atheist to stomach. Sovereign man hopes to first negate but eventually become indifferent to God. He no longer derives strength, as many atheisms do, from a rejection of God.

*

Sade completes the project of Western metaphysics by 'founding man's sovereignty on the transcending power of negation, a power that depends in no way upon the objects that it destroys, which in order to destroy them, does not even suppose their existence beforehand'. But then, as Blanchot argues, he goes one further. Sade rejects the idea of God as the 'inexpiable fault of man, his original sin, the proof of his emptiness.'[43] Sade again:

> The very conceiving of this so infinitely disgusting phantom is, I confess it, the one wrong I am unable to forgive man. I excuse him all his whims, his ironies, and his eccentricities, I sympathize with all his frailties, but I cannot smile tolerantly upon the lunacy that could erect this monster, I do not pardon man for having himself wrought those religious chains which have so dreadfully hobbled him and for having crept despicably forward, eyes downcast and neck stretched forth, to receive the shameful collar manufactured only by his own stupidity. There would be no end to it, Juliette, were I to give vent to all the horror waked in me by the execrable doctrine based upon a God's existence; mere mention of him rouses my ire, when I hear his name pronounced I seem to see all around me the palpitating shades of all those woebegone creatures this abominable opinion has slaughtered on the face of the earth. Those ghosts cry out beseechingly to me, they supplicate me to make use of all I have been endowed with of force and ingenuity to erase from the souls of my brethren the idea of the revolting chimera which has brought such rue into the world.[44]

The chimera that Sade rejects is 'what justifies and authorizes' those crimes he imagines, 'for we cannot be too forceful in our efforts to annihilate a being who is willing to bow down and prostrate himself before God'.[45]

The idea of God reduces man to nothingness, Sade perceives, since man conceives of himself as owing everything to that idea however vaguely it may be expressed. Indeed, the idea of God derives its strength from the fact that God must remain unknown, from the fact that "his ineffable ways surpass understanding, that he waxes wroth as soon as anyone has the temerity to pry into his secrets".[46] Those seeking mastery have, then, no option but to make God manifest, to give definite form to man's conception of divine sovereignty and reign over men like Gods. To remove the last vestiges of religious faith, Sadean man 'momentarily becomes God, so that, when in his presence, other men become inconsequential and then realize exactly to what extent a being before God is sheer nothingness'. 'Being God can only mean one thing: crushing men, annihilating creation.'[47] Thus Sadean man finally destroys any last vestige of God by assuming His image. At the same time he destroys men by acting out the consequences of their image of themselves as reflected in their conception of God. He shows how in creating God they inaugurated their own destruction.

*

In man's conception of God Sade 'hates the nothingness of man – who created such a master for himself'. Though Sade's characters would temporarily 'work with God to sanction this nothingness' – to express the destructive logic in the idea of God and bring it to its conclusion – they will not become Godlike for more time than is necessary.[48] Sade eventually gives up even hating God, so Blanchot's argues, for in hating God Sade affirms God by negation. His hatred of God must finally mature until it 'liberates hate from God'.[49] Sade's hate becomes 'too great to be contained by just one object'. He identifies instead with that 'spirit of destruction' he associates with

Nature.[50] Yet Nature too becomes unbearable. By aligning himself with Nature, Sade finds himself 'constantly confronted' with its 'insurmountable and sovereign presence'.[51] Nature as conceived by Man, dooms us to a pursuit we can never fulfil. We are formed, Sade tells us, so that we would wish to outrage her, but as Nature herself is the spirit of destruction, there is no outrage, no act of destruction, that can escape her embrace. As the libertine Pope explains, addressing Nature:

> Thou, unreasoning and reasonless force of which I find myself the involuntary result, Thou who hurled me into this world with the desire that I offend Thee, and who hast however denied me the means to do so, inspire in my blazing soul those crimes which would serve Thee better than these poor melancholy things Thou hast put inside my reach... When I have exterminated all the creatures that cover the earth, still shall I be far from my mark, since I shall have merely served Thee, O unkind Mother, for it is to vengeance I aspire, vengeance for what, whether through stupidity or malice, Thou doest to men in never furnishing them the means to translate fairly into deeds the appalling desires Thou dost ever rouse in them.[52]

Sadean man 'gradually becomes aggravated' by Nature.[53] His sovereignty will bear no comparison to its supremacy. Nature too must studied, and subjected to libertine probing. The study of Nature helps destroy our last presumptions concerning Man, God, Justice and so on; it is part of the process of their negation. The libertine must engage in "incessant, unwearying study of her; only by probing into her furthermost recesses may one finally destroy the last of one's misconceptions".[54] But the study of Nature also allows for the possibility of her own negation, or so the most accomplished libertine comes to believe. And so we find imagined a great cataclysm that would destroy the very laws of Nature. Sade imagines an engineer of such accomplishment that he creates a machine to 'pulverize the universe'.[55] Though even this, for Sade, would not suffice.

*

By his imagined defeat of Nature, Sade's mastery once again becomes dependent upon, and presumes the existence of, that which it destroys. What he 'pursued by pushing the spirit of negation to its limit is sovereignty'.[56] He sought after a sovereign mastery which creates and destroys without appeal. Through the pursuit of mastery and after so much destruction, Sade eventually sacrifices mastery, travelling beyond good and evil, and beyond value itself. He realises it will not suffice to ensure the other is reduced to nothing through its destruction. For, as Klossowski argued in *Sade My Neighbour*, 'if the other is *nothing* for me... I am not only *nothing* for him but also *nothing* before my own consciousness – and in fact that consciousness is no longer still *mine*'.[57] Here we are left with the last effects of *Sade's Reason*. At its extreme realisation, mastery (and hence education) destroys itself; it reduces sovereign man to nothing since if he is something he must exist in dependent relation to something else. We arrive at the 'negation of destruction itself'.[58]

*

The wilful destruction of objects belies the dependence of the destroyer on those things he annihilates. What better way to remove that dependence, Sade decides, than to depreciate it by becoming apathetic to destruction itself. Now the simple 'quantity of the objects sacrificed, becomes the object of these acts'. Deriving little from their destruction, these acts being too numerous to count or even notice, the 'reality of the other and of the self are dissolved'.[59] As Horkheimer and Adorno put it: little but a 'tense, purposive bustle prevails' in which 'no moment is unused, no body orifice neglected, no function left inactive'.[60] The libertine disappears 'in an endless reiteration of acts'.[61] He romps without purpose, remaining active for no other reason. Like today's educator, yet shorn of all romantic illusion, sovereign man in his last iteration operates 'devoid of any substantial goals',[62] everything he touches is apprehended 'in terms of manipulation and administration.'[63] As Sade's Chief of Police declares:

> It does indeed seem that the lamp of reason does not begin to enlighten us until such time as we are no longer able to profit from its rays, and not before stupidity has been added to stupidity that we arrive at the discovery of the source of all that ignorance has caused us to commit.[64]

Let us treat this remark with the seriousness it deserves. Once Sade's reason has run its full course and mastery has emptied itself of all content, there is nothing left to say. After so many lessons we find ourselves stripped bare, piling stupidity upon stupidity. At its limit, this is what education for mastery becomes.

Mastery or Failure

Sade's direction of travel is also our own, insofar as we too suffer the effects of 'European nihilism'.[65] But our collective travel is less deliberate: we kill Man, God and Nature without always fully intending to. This killing of each is built into the pursuit of mastery that we (unlike Sade) disavow. Sade only brings to the surface that brutalism inherent in Western education, which negates and negates monstrously in order to affirm. If this tendency were fully acknowledged, if the grotesque nature of our dream, our pursuit of mastery were fully manifested, we might develop the strength to reject it as our educational objective. And not by returning to that dirty compromise of mastery through enslavement, which kills, though it does so quietly. Rather we might pursue its opposite, which is failure, a failure to master others and ourselves.

*

Mastery or failure, these are the options given us by education. Mastery is promised through a sleight of hand that prevents its delivery (we become enslaved to the pursuit of something that is rarely, if ever, realised), whilst failure is guaranteed. Educational failure is far more common and systematically produced than we would like to admit. In short, if one did not fail, another would not succeed. Outside Sade's grasp, educational mastery is only ever relative, never absolute, though it still brings destruction in its wake. Educational mastery appears in a reduced form, where the mastery of those who succeed is dependent on the existence of those multitudes that fail. We are in a position similar to that of the debauched libertine still reliant on the "pleasure of comparison." Educational success remains dependent on educational failure, on negation. We are not simply waiting for the 'right' pedagogy to be applied 'successfully' so that failure can be removed.[66] Once described as the 'traumatic real' of contemporary education, failure belies the barbarism of educational mastery and the fantasy of an educational good.[67] In a perverse cycle of self-affirmation, education is offered as the solution to the problem, that of systemic failure, which education creates. Failure is the necessary consequence of that nihilism which attaches us to promises that are never delivered, which makes us its inevitable disappointments. The educated nihilist would not retreat from failure, then. This figure would not seek to heal education of that affliction, since failure constitutes education. Even for the educated nihilist this is difficult to admit. It really is traumatic for those wedded by constitution to an ideology of educational success.

*

Our options are limited by our histories. And they appear radically opposed. We affirm mastery or we pursue its opposite. Rejecting mastery, we could embrace failure instead, learning to fail better. We could seek to fail without appeal, failing on our own terms. But *can* we fail without appeal? It seems unlikely. For our failures to be affirmed in their own right, they would need to fall outside the shadow of a promised mastery. As we plummet downwards, we would confront that devil, the 'Spirit of Heaviness' through which 'all things fall'.[68] We would laugh heartily at that metaphysical ghost, which nihilism produces and has us suffer. We would confront that spirit and understand how it was first and forever since conjured by man. Confronted by things that will no longer be suspended aloft. These things fall, we fall with them. This fallout we perceive as the necessary outcome of that unnecessary belief in spectral things, ideas, Gods.

*

Our affirmation of failure would be deliberate, giving expression to our nihilism, revealing its downward tendencies. We would no longer kill Man, God and Nature, or this outcome would at least become less inevitable, since mastery, and education too, would no longer be revered.

VIII

A MODERN FETISH

Incessant Motion
With modern science the dead acquired degrees of vitality. The boundary between life and death became uncertain as vital signs were observed in the deceased. Better still, they were put to use, as body parts were consumed by the living. Seventeenth century doctors noted a range of unusual phenomena: The corpse retained a 'remnant of life', where some claimed the dead body of a victim bleeds profusely when placed in the presence of the murderer.[1] Continued movement was recorded along with perspiration and the growth of hair, nails and teeth. Erections were reported on hanged men and dead soldiers. Cadavers emitted 'sounds like the squealing of pigs from the depths of their graves'. When the graves were opened it was reported that the dead had 'devoured their shrouds or their clothing'. Was this an omen of plague? Were these 'noisy and hungry corpses'

natural or diabolical phenomena? Either way, a transformation had occurred. The corpse was given its own sensibility.[2]

*

Vestiges of life could be harvested for the living. A cadaver's sweat was considered a good remedy for haemorrhoids and tumours. The still-warm hand of a corpse might cure diseased areas. Dead body parts could be used to heal living ones, like for like. The soil of graves, especially of hanged men, was rich in therapeutic properties. The most fertile soil contained bones. The ashes of 'happily married couples and lovers' could be taken as an aphrodisiac.[3] Effectively, the dead body was becoming productive, both as source of knowledge and source of material. From here it was a short step to treating the living body as one treats the dead, from dreams of animating the dead (a modern Prometheus), to institutes for animating the living through artificial technique. A disciplinary regime was in the making. It produced not simply the mechanical movements but also the 'life-force' of the living.[4] This regime developed its own romance, as death acquired its own beauty. Schools were filled with pained desire, as martyred saints adorned churches with 'macabre eroticism'.[5] Complete with aching romance, both productive and lost: this is our new order.

*

Education has long been obsessed with death, operating variously as a self-denying bodily ordinance, of marginal, perhaps supine, supplicatory eroticism. Yet today the scheme is adjusted. The bodily denials of the death-bound educator – those denials we inherit from ancient Greece – have been augmented. We encounter bodies amassed and in motion. Education confronts us with ceaseless activity as it shuffles forth without direction or strength, our only consolation being the sensation it gives of incessant friction.[6] Yet despite our weakened condition, the romantic educator can still demand the odd, temporary interruption, and mount the occasional revolt. We still have the affective resources to appreciate the perversity of our shifting about. But we are carried away nonetheless, yielding to sensations of movement.

*

The problem for today's Cynic, for a returned Diogenes, is not that life has been denied in any straightforward sense, or emptied of meaning. Rather, meaning is now dependent on the body. The Cynic confronts bodies in ceaseless motion, each bearing witness to its own existence.[7]

*

In its latest manifestation, education allows weak cynicism to fester and multiply. We must insist if nothing else on the uselessness of this breed of cynicism. It risks nothing but remains open to seduction. It appears to reject everything but remains susceptible to the allure of redemption. Today's cynic may be withdrawn and dejected but is prone to a superficial romance, to a frottage with educational ideals that gives temporary relief. Education becomes a fetish.

*

Education is that kind of fetish which functions best when left unquestioned. The fervour with which we pursue education is proportionate to our ignorance of its nature. Those who ask the simple question "What is education?" so flaunt common protocol they are met with embarrassment: "Do they really mean to admit, quite so openly and to those of us who know, that they have no idea?" Silence ensues. Following which the security of an assumed answer is shored up by the collective inertia of those refusing to ask the question.

As Universal Good

Education has become victim of its universality. Before education became an inalienable right, that thing everyone must have, it had some definite content, specific to the context in which it was expressed. For the Roman elite, education represented a form of training for those hoping to operate within the higher machinery of Empire. For the early Christian, education represented a form of spiritual training for those hoping to ward off the devil. Education effectively changed definition across contexts, being free of the expectation that, as universal right, it must transcend them all and be applicable to each.

*

Once universalised, education stood for all activities that could be gathered under its umbrella. It even applied to anyone 'left outside' – where all activities could be measured according to their educational value. Under these conditions, education would no longer have any kind of definite content. Here it approximates the commodity fetish described by Marx, itself an effect of generalisation. The commodity fetish appears following transition from pre-capitalist societies – where there was no need for labour and its products to assume a 'fantastic form' since they existed in localised relations of dependence – to capitalist societies where labour and its products became necessary abstractions.[8] By analogy, 'education' only became a fantastical ideal, and hence a fetish, once it was necessary to abstract education across diverse contexts, establishing a principle of equivalence (everything is educational) across unequal contexts (education is doing very different things, to different people). The universality of education could only take hold on the condition its variety was provisionally ignored, on the premise that all variations are placed behind a principle of equivalence. Only then could the idea of education as a universal right make sense. Crucially, there is no commitment here to making education the same for all. Its universality is only expressed as an abstraction. This gives birth to the fatuous idea that education can be measured across contexts, that you can have an objectively 'good' or 'bad' school, teacher, university or curriculum.

*

Education has long been oriented to a transcendent educational 'good'. For centuries, there was an awkward relation between educational practices and their ultimate objective, an educational good forever to be deferred. But in each case the deferral was given appropriate content and a clear enough rationale. For the Roman tutor, the promise of an educational good was attached to the common practice of *paideia*, without which the aristocrat could not function. For the Christian bishop, the promise of an educational good was attached to the labour of securing the soul's place in heaven. In modernity, however, once education is universalised, the educational good it promises must be relevant to all contexts. We are left with the following predicament: If we seek to uncover what education really is, perhaps in an attempt to better defend it from attack, we must either radically limit our scope in order assert that it is something particular, or we must return to pre-modern definitions of education that were limited by the specific contexts which gave birth to them. Each attempt to find and defend contemporary education fails to understand that its lack of content is precisely what defines it.

*

Today's educators are expected to be the bearers of a thing that only makes sense so long as it remains in motion. By analogy, the commodity Marx describes in *Capital* has little intrinsic worth beyond its immediate use-value. It achieves universal value only as a set of relations, established by those who act before thinking, by those who assume value exists and base their actions upon the common assumption of its objectivity.[9] In a similar way, modern education is given its content though the ceaseless activity of educators who begin only with the deed, assuming that education has independent worth beyond the immediate instances of its use.[10] This is difficult to recognise since, as Marx put it, 'the movement through which this process has been mediated vanishes in its own result, leaving no trace behind'.[11] We are left, quite simply, with the conviction that education as a universal concept, already exists before us. We refuse to see the alternative, which is to say that the value of education is produced because it is pursued. This is a riddle. It still has us in its grasp.

*

The commodification of education is much bemoaned. Under the name of that abstract foe neoliberalism, a market logic invests our educational institutions. Accordingly today's student is lamented for treating her education as a commodity. She is deplored for treating her educators as its vendors. She expects, so they say, to get a return on her investment. In response educational institutions adopt the language of the marketplace. They are sold and sell themselves as commodities, dressing their windows, maintaining the brand. They insist that their workforce understands itself, and its relations, as already branded goods. This situation is much scoffed at by those of greater refinement and with longer memories, who consider themselves and their wares to be above and beyond commodification. These noble souls insist they are no mere shopkeepers of knowledge. They will not have their efforts reduced, as if they were so many pieces of merchandise with a given price. But the commodification of education is much older than these educated critics suspect. Moreover, it has long operated in reverse, issuing *from* the romantic attachments of those educators who place education upon a pedestal, and generalise, universalise its worth. Since education became a universal signifier, and so had no specific purchase on a particular educational reality, all moments could in principle be packaged, and considered in terms of their educational value. Education, as an abstract signifier, became the universal money form that could be used as a principle of exchange converting anything into an educational commodity. Education became the universal, empty signifier through which the value of all formative moments could be expressed. Everything was now in principle educational, where educational moments only varied in terms of their relative value, some having more than others. The recent and more obvious commodification of our educational institutions, our schools and universities, is only a belated and inverted realisation of that logic. And this situation is to their benefit, since today's institutions would stretch any narrow definition of education to breaking point. A broad if not empty signifier allows institutional life to become decidedly cynical and yet still be called 'educational'. These institutions are happily promiscuous in that respect. Nothing can take away their educational credentials however grubby their operations.

The Educated Critic
Educated critics have no idea how impotent they become, destroying connections with practice as they retreat into abstraction. They find security in their expertise, in their idealism, in their capacity for intellectualised contempt, in educated diversions as frightfully nebulous as they are reassuringly dense. But our critics are rejected themselves with equal if not greater force by the instrumental rationality within which they operate. They are largely ignored by an educational system that is cynically performed to monstrous effect. The story of modernity is their story, that of the 'disembodiment of knowledge', of its 'divorce from the knower', from the moral commitments of those able to draw from a shared morality.[12] Our critics have little to contribute, having no shared system of value, and no agreed educational project to which they may appeal. They are without the means to interrupt those morbid proceedings from which they devoutly recoil. All we have is a critic's recital of woeful notes, a mere tuning up of instruments that convey little but toneless devotion. They expel air, hot air: that is all.

*

A new breed of moralist would bring the 'intensity of a moral performance' to the flagging project of the educational critic.[13] This moralist would assert the impossibility of our existing moral order, and our impossible existence within it. In Cynic terms, the challenge to live 'like a dog, that is to say, in rupture with society'.[14] One does not observe remotely from above or below, but seeks exposure, adopting a perilous stance, open to biting and being bitten. Intellectual problems are indulged accordingly, only if they are felt.

*

To make a life the test of its critique is to risk that life. Ancient Cynics have been widely misunderstood in this respect, so odd do they appear by contrast to the reserved, enlightened critic. Cynic aggression has been interpreted as if it were a species of simple insolence, or at best a form of 'existential self-assertion in the face of annihilating power'.[15] The Cynic does nothing but gives vent to his libidinous energies, so it goes. The Cynic protest is just a barbaric cry, a futile plea for freedom. There is nothing worth repeating here... That is the diagnosis of prissy folk. They cannot see the 'patient labour'[16] that lies behind each act of Cynic subversion. There is no discipline more exacting than that of the Cynic, whose rebellions are not at random. They are situated with care, designed to confront those 'principles to which society pays lip service'.[17] They lay bare such principles, twist and contort them. Each Cynic revolt attempts to refashion how we are fashioned as self-asserting subjects wedded despite ourselves to systems that define our being. Or to switch terminology, one might frame this as a question of desubjectification. It is a matter of confronting the educational subject, or making that subject confront itself, as we labour to experience 'something leading to its actual destruction, its decomposition, its explosion' and perhaps 'conversion into something else'.[18] A Cynic strategy in part, here too is the gist of Foucault's critical ethos. In response to the complaint his work had a 'paralyzing' effect on its readers, Foucault remarked, 'this very reaction proves that the work was successful'.[19] Following an honest reading of *Discipline and Punish* a correctional officer or social worker should expect to be at a loss, no longer able to rely so easily upon those assumptions that make up his or her professional self. An educator might experience similar paralysis.

*

It is assumed that all 'great thinkers' deserve commentary. For how could academics not generate commentaries, critiques and compendia of their illustrious predecessors? And yet, when approaching a thinker such as Foucault we might wonder if he needs such accompaniment. Admittedly his work benefits from a certain amount of guided digestion and elaboration. But here it is hardly left wanting. Foucault-related scholarship abounds. We should pay attention to the tone of this scholarship, often at odds with the deliberate 'production of estrangement' to which Foucault aspired.[20] Most of it is already too familiar. Too predictably Foucauldian. By contrast Foucault offered a detailed but disruptive reading of texts, destabilizing those aspects of the present most readily taken as its givens. This was intended to open the present to the possibility of its transformation. In pursuing his objective Foucault would necessarily appear odd, if not untimely, perhaps unreasonable. Hence those who read Foucault best are not simply informed by his work, they are unsettled by it. But the typical scholar is characteristically and temperamentally opposed to the untimely meditations, the 'inopportune and vigorous contemplations' of a thinker who, at his best, overturned those frameworks we most take for granted.[21] This was 'an uneasy and restless' activity, as Foucault's interminable self-adjustments and restatements of purpose bear witness.[22] The danger with conventional scholarship, with the whole industry now surrounding Foucault's work, is that it buries this restless ethic under the weight of its commentaries. Nietzsche bemoaned that scholarly habit, which serves to destroy the extraordinary impulse echoed in the work of the philosopher under study. Through excessively scrupulous enquiries the scholar unwittingly helps 'to break or – even better! – to loosen every tensed bow', with 'deference, with a gentle hand, to be sure – in friendly sympathy *loosen it.*'[23] For Nietzsche the choice was obvious. To the extent academic philosophy is overrun by a scholarly impulse, the 'true philosopher' must today live "unphilosophically' and 'unwisely' and above all *imprudently*...continually risking himself'.[24] The problem with so much work taking inspiration from Foucault, and Nietzsche for that matter, is that it entails little risk, causes little disruption, and invites little action.

An Odd Beast Indeed

For the Cynic *parrhesiast*, scholarship is an alien activity. The parrhesiast obeys a very different regime of truth.[25] As Foucault argues, for this 'mode of verediction' or truth-telling to occur,[26] the subject who speaks the truth 'must be taking some kind of risk...a risk which concerns his relationship with the person to whom he is speaking'. With courage the parrhesiast will take the risk 'of offending the other person, of irritating him, of making him angry and provoking him to conduct which may even be extremely violent'.[27] For the scholar this announces the opposite. It signifies the departure of truth before a reign of force.

*

Not all parrhesiasts are outsiders. For some frank speech involved a pact with the powerful, where the parrhesiast becomes a necessary figure in the King's Counsel. Here the parrhesiast still demonstrates courage by telling the truth, but he does so expectantly. To participate, 'the person to whom this *parrhesia* is addressed will have to demonstrate his greatness of soul by accepting being told the truth'.[28] Such truth is uttered in earnest, and in this respect is entirely opposed to the art of rhetoric. In antiquity, rhetoric enabled the person speaking 'to say something which may not be what he thinks at all, but whose effect will be to produce convictions' or instil certain beliefs in the person to whom he speaks. Rhetoric established 'a constraining bond between what is said and the person or persons to whom it is said'.[29] Here it is the exact opposite of parrhesia, which risks the bond between parrhesiast and audience. The parrhesiast may provoke anger, turn friend into enemy, 'arouse the hostility of the city, or, if he is speaking the truth to a bad and tyrannical sovereign, he may provoke vengeance and punishment'. He may even 'pay with his life for the truth he has told'.[30] Hence the Roman tutor, in part parrhesiast but also philosopher, also learnt to seduce. Through seduction, through a common belief in education, he would re-establish the very bond his advice put in peril.

*

The parrhesiast must contend with other rival truth-tellers, such as the prophet who transmits the wisdom of others, or the sage who transmits his own. The prophet's posture is one of mediation, often transmitting the word of God and always addressing his audience with 'a truth that comes from elsewhere'.[31] The prophet is intermediary in another sense too, serving as a point of connection between the present and its prophetic future. The parrhesiast, by contrast, makes no attempt to help people somehow step beyond 'some threshold in the ontological structure of the human being and of time, which separates them from their future'. At most, the parrhesiast 'helps them in their blindness' seeking to unveil reality in all its coarseness, so that it may be better acted upon. This truth-teller avoids the characteristic obscurity of prophetic speech, with its divine riddles, seeking to say things as clearly and directly as possible, without any 'disguise or rhetorical embellishment'. The objective is to speak in such a way that one's words strike home with maximum force...[32] The posture of the sage with regard to truth-telling is very different. Characteristically the sage considers the very nature of things in grand abstraction. Comfortable in his obscurity, the sage feels no compulsion to speak and give others the benefit of his wisdom. By contrast, the parrhesiast must always speak, favouring only knowledge that is directly and urgently applicable to one's life.[33] The parrhesiast has no time for grandiose ideas that lesser mortals might be invited to contemplate. Rather the parrhesiast seeks to demonstrate, and encourages his audience to discover, what they are... Modern teaching occupies a far more restricted regime of truth. As a profession, teachers and academics tend to evaluate things very differently, seeking to transmit approved truths (known as curricula), or at least gain approval by consent for any scrap of 'new' knowledge they manage to produce. The teacher 'establishes, or at any rate hopes to establish a bond of shared knowledge, of heritage, of tradition, and possibly also of personal recognition' with the student body. Teaching becomes a matter of passing things on without taking too much risk in truth-telling. A teacher of this kind is 'linked to a whole weight of tradition' that bears down upon the profession and lends it its seriousness.[34] In direct contrast to the parrhesiast, for whom the most pertinent truths are the most dangerous, the teacher and academic takes the highest truths to be those associated with the greatest safety. They are least contestable and hence most worthy of inclusion in the curriculum. In effect, the more secure, the more true. To suggest with Cynic malice that teachers or academics might better pursue untimely ideas, measuring their value by the jeopardy they entail, is to invite these same educators to drop entirely out of one regime and land in another. On the whole they would fail – if indeed they could be convinced to make the attempt in the first place. But educators are not bound inexorably to their favoured mode of truth-telling. It would be a mistake to claim that for all teachers and academics truth-telling is always associated with security and consensus. The 'modes of veredicition' Foucault outlines intermingle, and so the teacher's mode of truth-telling might find itself combined at times with other modes. In the traditional university, for example, the teacher's duty to transmit heritage, pass down learning and ways of thinking, is found in combination with a sage-like figure. That is, it is embodied in the old-school academic who speaks of grand generalities. Unlike the teacher, this academic feels under no compulsion to share this wisdom, or at least will only divulge his or her knowledge when it suits (or under duress, when forced to teach the undergraduates).[35] Equally, teachers now abound who consider it their calling to teach their students to 'think independently', 'become autonomous' and so on. Yet these teachers and their academic supporters characteristically give little attention to the role of teacher as exemplar in this respect. It remains the case that the pedagogue's approach to truth is rarely if ever combined with that of the parrhesiast, where all that is shared between these positions is the duty to speak. We should not underestimate the extent to which educators are wedded to a mode of truth-telling that remains bounded, that does not risk the subjectivity of the educator. If realised, the Cynical educator and parrhesiast would be an odd beast indeed, but a beast of this world nonetheless.

*

As a fetish education persists. Not simply does it habituate the educator to a mode of truth telling that entails little personal risk, and hence encourages a point of view that will not risk taking up a position of truth *against* education. More obliquely, education will not be given up because there is little to abandon. To give up on education is not to risk destroying an edifice, it is to discover no edifice exists. More modestly, it is to recognise that, as its mission, *telos* or guiding ideal, this edifice is made of fine-grained but dead materials, falling back as soon as shored up. How could you take a position against that?

*

Educators may shy away from risking their profession. It may be their habit to proceed apace with mouths agape, eyes fixed shut and limbs in motion; feeding the former with materials grasped by the latter, only making for a greater hunger. Educators are bound to a situation whereby the educational *telos* of modernity is not so much hollow, as given substance and value through the exhaustion of its labour force. In Marx's terms, educational labour is a 'commodity whose use-value possesses the peculiar property of being a source of value', whose 'consumption is therefore itself an objectification'.[36] That is to say, the value of educational work is only realised through its consumption, where educators themselves are always the first consumer. Educators are bound to defend precisely that which drains them of vitality. But they are not, for all that, suffering for want of an alternative. Educators of the cynical kind may be right in refusing as futile any attempt to reverse or radically overhaul a system whose inertia is centuries old. But Cynical educators may nonetheless become active in an attempt to hasten its downgoing. It is worth noting here that the idea of impossible suicide is in one respect continuous with the history of education. This form of educational militancy is as moribund as its comparatively mundane educational cousins. Here we have another form of educated denial, though admittedly more radically nihilistic than its cousins, those existing (and already death-bound) traditions of Western education. And so again, I am not suggesting a radical departure from education as if one could escape its confines by decree. Rather, I invite here a radicalisation of its existing tendencies. This is not prompted by some vitalism, where against this educational foe we glorify life, fight for life and so on. This is not a matter of life versus education.

Consumptive Educators

'Education is sick' – this declaration of ill-health is commonplace today. But I have a second declaration in mind. Rather more deviously, it suggests those declaring ill-health, and those agreeing, are equally sick. In response, educators and educated people alike will likely deny they are similarly far-gone. Or, more to the point, they will acknowledge the sickness of education in a way that affirms the educated self. For are not those who spot the sickness, those who are most refined?

*

'Your sickness can be your crowning' – the death-bound hope of the educated person. To the Romantic poet, consumption (in the tubercular sense) was for a time the most 'alluring' of all diseases.[37] In the early nineteenth century it was, as Alexandre Dumas put it a little wryly, 'the fashion to suffer from the lungs; everybody was a consumptive, poets especially; it was good form to spit blood after each emotion that was at all sensational, and to die before reaching the age of thirty'.[38] In the poetic imagination at least, tubercular consumption held the promise of a beautiful death; it was portrayed as the 'glamorous disease' of the genius.[39] Medical and literary opinion seemed to agree: the consumptive poet was afflicted by 'enhanced sensibility to the point of excessive suffering when in contact with the rough, 'insensible' world'.[40] Over-stimulated, the consumptive burned too brightly, exhausting vital energies at an unsustainable rate. Fatal genius was the outcome of an over-exerted mind. The consumptive poet wasted away: emaciated and with deathly pallor, reaching towards genius, bright one moment, dead the next. Two centuries on, the suffering of the romantic educator bears comparison, as this educator strains towards an educational good that is otherwise denied by a harsh, insensible reality. The romantic educator is in some weakened sense, a martyr to the sickness of education. Seduced by the romance of consumption, romantic educators seem to realise despite themselves that the very disease that drains them of vitality, this wasting disease that exhausts them as a labour force, is the source of all value in education. It is as if their wilful exhaustion were expressive of all that remains good about education. In their hyperactivity resides their love, for they only allowed themselves to put up with so much overwork, so many hours, so much stress for so long, out of love for what they do. Exhaustion through education is the inevitable outcome today of a love of education. The educator is truest to education when most done in.

*

The virtues of a consumptive death were so exalted it became decorative and lyrical, almost metaphysical. Being a disease of the lungs, those loftier parts of the human being, this ailment had its own nobility, rendering it distinct from afflictions of the lower regions. Those other ailments were mere diseases of the body, whereas consumption was expressive of the soul.[41] It demanded the use of privileges only available to the wealthy and refined. It required rest, retreat and travel. Symptomatic of excessive passion, of an over-refined sensibility, consumption was treated by therapies that would allow such ardour to be expressed in a more controlled and gentle environment. Two centuries on, the educator is prone to a similar romance. Those most committed to educational redemption are drawn, sometimes despite themselves, to want to inherit such indulgences. After all, the survival of education is at stake. Afflicted by their zealous attachment to education, by a desire for the realisation of an as yet unrealised educational good, by a passion for education that can, we are led to believe, only just be contained; they would have themselves housed liberally in a privileged and protected environment, so they might safely luminesce without burning up. Brimming with enthusiasm, exuberant, almost tearful, this educator begs our indulgence, pleading for an educational environment that is safe and comfortable, one that guarantees the survival of the educator, and the survival of an educational art that is always vulnerable and needs protection. The alternative for a consumptive and passionate educator such as this is relapse, decay, ultimately death, where the life at stake is not simply that of the educator but that of refined sensibility itself. But these are mere diversions. Despite all entreaties, all appeals for therapy and respite, the consumptive educator remains bound to a consumptive death. Do not be distracted by the exuberance of our most romantic educators, or by the educator's claim to health and productivity. Death beckons.

*

The consumptive educator almost desires to waste away. This wasting disease has come to represent the apotheosis of one's career. It is expressive of one's commitment to education, poetry, culture and refinement. And for all that, it is profoundly nihilistic (in the weak sense) drawing meaning and purpose from its own enfeebled destruction. When the value of education is expressed only through the determined exhaustion of its labour force, it becomes a matter of strenuous self-expression, little more. The persistence of educated conceit in a landscape so broken may well disturb us, but it should not lead to any kind of persecution. Persecution gives its object the 'appearance of honourableness' – it bestows on it the 'fascination of martyrdom'.[42] Besides, is the 'martyrdom' of the educator even an argument? Is the educator's sacrifice-by-exhaustion an argument for education? Must we refute it as if it were?

*

The educated Cynic admits that our claim to educated refinement has no independent standing. It stands by comparison only. Education depends on those debased educational realities that educated people bemoan. Our refinement and our conceit relies on this contrast. Against it they gain relief. Educated people maintain that distinction.

*

We are ill with education, there is no denying it. Our educated conceit *is* our illness. Our task, perhaps the task defining our present, is to focus with courage on that morbid truth. It is to experience, for so long as we can bear, this sickness stripped of its consumptive romance.

The Cynical Educator

IX

THE ABSURD

Artificial Brutalities
Diogenes was asked how he would like to be buried. 'On my face' he replied, since 'after a little time down will be converted into up'.[1] Even Diogenes is too optimistic for us now.

*

The educated nihilist is schooled to the point of revolt, and reads Nietzsche for signs of conduct. For all her wilful distortions Nietzsche's sister could at least see the logic in that: "Dear, dear Clara *tell no one...* Fritz has become different, he *is* just like his books".[2]

*

Nietzsche's first book, *The Birth of Tragedy* tears away at the brutal idealism of Greek philosophy and all that comes after. However, 'questionable', however *'impossible'* his book appeared in retrospect, in its grip was a 'problem with horns'.[3] That is, the legacy of Greek metaphysics, and what Nietzsche called 'Socratism'.[4] This originated the belief that despite our ignorance everything is knowable, and hence *teachable.* [5] From Socrates onwards, so it goes, nothing satisfies the appetite of education. Insatiable, greedy for knowledge, knowing no bounds, education has fitted a gastric band. An equally Socratic tendency to constrain the appetites pacifies those hungering for education. It draws boundaries between and within them, inside which they are to achieve 'self-knowledge and moderation'.[6] For Nietzsche: 'All of our educational methods take their bearings from this ideal'.[7] Hence *The Birth of Tragedy* indicts Western education to its core.

*

Greek tragedy is not to be confused with that other tragic experience more familiar to us now. At its most decadent, misfortunes are greedily embraced as opportunities to display refined, compassionate sensibilities. Typically bourgeois, as Camus observed, these moderns '*need* tragedy' in a different way – 'it's their little transcendence, their apéritif' – used to 'bestir themselves' and their finer emotions.[8] Nietzsche preferred the pre-Socratic Greeks. Less self-indulgent, their experience of tragedy was of a different order. It issued from a horrific realisation that the world not only lacks meaning but is profoundly indifferent to human suffering. The pre-Socratic Greeks had seen into the abyss and perceived well enough that beneath it all, stripped of mythologies and consolations, existence is horrifically banal, formless. Nietzsche indicts everything since Socrates for papering over that profound indifference. For denying the existential horror it produces. Education, philosophy, culture, religion – these are all too many distractions. Whilst Greek tragedy afforded a 'metaphysical consolation'[9] of sorts, allowing its pre-Socratic auditors to approach reality through its representation in art, *and survive the encounter,* its influence would not last. Tragic theatre was destroyed and replaced by the cheerful optimism of a Socratic quest. Following Nietzsche, 'Socratism' is a distraction we can no longer afford. This cultural bequeathment of the metaphysical Greeks operates as a blight upon us, the extent of which is only just becoming apparent.

*

'The blight that lies dormant in the womb of theoretical culture is gradually beginning to frighten modern man', Nietzsche writes. Man 'casts uneasily around in the stores of experience for remedies to ward off the danger *without quite believing in their efficacy*'.[10] In Nietzsche's first book we find already portrayed the restless subjectivity of the modern cynic. We encounter 'theoretical man' who trots out remedies as today's educator trots out techniques, cheerfully forlorn, weakly pessimistic, but committed nonetheless.

The Tragedy of Education

Despite the aporia and inherent difficulties of *The Birth of Tragedy,* that impossible book whose *non-sequiturs* later scholars would almost, but never quite, bet their life on – we begin to imagine its consequences for education. A distraction from the brutality of existence, education introduces brutalities of its own. The indifference of the world is replaced by the moral imperium of education, far from indifferent when it comes to human lives. Despite its consolations, despite pasting meaning and order into existence, education attaches to that existence its impossible excess: the unearthly goal of wisdom. In its modern form this pursuit is reduced to the equally specious though decidedly less noble quest for educational success. Other close associates include innovation, creativity and the cultivation of an aspiring, entrepreneurial spirit. To a degree the effect is similar. These distinctly late modern goals continue to domesticate us with the sense, when measured against them, there is something lacking we must work to fulfil. But to add insult to injury, our educational objectives are no longer seriously attached to a project seeking after their realisation, promising our fulfilment. Without the accompaniment of a progressive metanarrative they exist marooned in the present. For Nietzsche, the existence of this educational dream world, and all those before it, is understandable, indeed necessary. Our weakness is that we allow it to consume us. In *The Birth of Tragedy* the pre-Socratic Greeks are presented as far less credulous. They do not escape entirely into equivalent distractions, but just enough to endure existence. The educator who takes inspiration from *The Birth of Tragedy* is always on the cusp of giving up on education entirely. As a friend of mine once said: 'I have always held on to the idea that it might all be for nothing, that education is just an exercise of power'. What intrigued me, was that he long drew *strength* from the very idea.

*

The pre-Socratic Greeks are credited with great sensitivity, for feeling and confronting the futility of their existence. According to Greek mythology, when the daemon Silenus was asked: 'What is the best and most desirable thing of all for mankind?' he answered; "The best of all things is something entirely outside your grasp: not to be born, not to *be*, to be *nothing*. But the second-best thing for you – is to die soon."[11] The early Greeks managed to overcome this demonic insight,[12] Nietzsche claims, without forgetting the deep pessimism it conveyed. They 'knew and felt the fears and horrors of existence: in order to be able to live at all they had to interpose the radiant dream-birth of the Olympians [and later, Greek tragedy] between themselves and those horrors'.[13] To live, the Greeks constructed a dreamworld, reflecting themselves in a 'higher sphere'[14] to cope with the 'primal suffering' below.[15] Unlike 'theoretical man' – which for Nietzsche stands for everything since Socrates – the pre-Socratic Greeks did not so easily mistake their reassuring fantasies for reality. Through tragedy they recognised the illusions they consoled themselves with were the products of 'eternal, primal suffering, the sole foundation of the world'.[16] Primal suffering is not considered evil. It is found at the origin of all human culture which seeks to redeem existence by giving it meaning: primal suffering is the wellspring of all beautiful distractions. A distinction that is crucial, having implications for all would-be educators and their educational consolations: it keeps all that is 'good' in culture and education in a state of suspense. It allows us to suspend judgement in a way that prevents us from fully believing education and culture might extinguish all that is 'bad', because bad or 'evil' things are acknowledged as the motor behind attempts to redeem existence in the first place. We have here, in other words, the makings of an eternally vigilant educational mindset which constantly interrogates the moral purpose of education. The history of education is darkened as its wellsprings are plumbed to their depths. The highest educational ideals are carefully and without demur located in the lowest, grubby moments of human intrigue. This genealogy of educational ideals digs away without indulging itself in the simple horror of its findings. The challenge is to occupy such a mindset, entertain such radical doubt and yet continue to educate.

*

Those taking lessons from *The Birth of Tragedy* must suffer its most fiendish insight. Nietzsche's 'cruellest moment', so it has been argued, was to recognise, and give voice to our absurd predicament. We realise with Nietzsche that we are 'intoxicated' by our metaphysical consolations, yet find ourselves able at the same time to recognise their bankruptcy.[17] We develop the 'horrible presentiment that metaphysical ways out might be void of meaning and that existence without a metaphysical overlay would be insufferable'.[18] Though we may think we turn unbearable conditions into bearable ones, we come to realise that we have not made 'unbearable circumstances bearable or even less bearable but only still more unbearable' as fabrications and lies.[19] The effect is deeply nauseating.

*

We have the following conundrum: Those perceiving how the 'horror and absurdity of existence'[20] is papered over by a world of illusion, those understanding these chaotic underpinnings, will 'consider it ludicrous or shameful that they should be expected to restore order to the chaotic world'.[21] Once they see through to the absurdity of life, and the absurdity of attempts to redeem it, they reach a kind of understanding that 'kills action'. Since 'action depends on a veil of illusion' which gives meaning to an indifferent universe.[22] Hence, the educator taking lessons from *The Birth of Tragedy* must just about maintain a belief in the civilizing illusion of education, if he or she is to continue to operate as an educator. This educator will realise nonetheless that the 'special stimulants'[23] of education, culture and civilization can become addictive, helping to paper over 'the repellence of the absurd'.[24] Searching for an alternative, Nietzsche put his faith in art (rather naively he later decided), yet also mentioned another release, *comedy.* [25] Perhaps then, today's educator should first admit the absurdity of the whole endeavour, and learn to laugh whilst laden. The educator's laugh would bring relief whilst expressing pain. Here we encounter 'the *comic* as a discharge of the nausea of absurdity'.[26] The Cynical educator learns the art of laughing as a letting of blood.

*

To those who find little worth in pessimism, especially educational pessimism, this is no laughing matter. For what is education without hope? Surely we must cure ourselves of all pessimism if we are to continue to educate? But what if Nietzsche was right to suggest, as he once did, that 'all pessimism (the inveterate evil of old idealists...) is thoroughly *cured* by falling ill'?[27] What if our pessimism is best approached by affirming it? By constitution educators are allergic to such suggestions. It makes no sense to wonder as Nietzsche once did if there could be a 'pessimism of *strength*'?[28] But we must insist on this question for that very reason and continue: Must pessimism always be associated with weakness and denial? Is pessimism in education necessarily deceitful, hiding from view educational values that could otherwise redeem it... and us? Or is educational *optimism* the greatest deceit? Certainly, pessimism is uncomfortable, excruciating at times as purgatives are. But it liberates us, if only in passing, from burdens of hope.

With Blistered Fingers

There is a suspicion I believe educators feel, if only fleetingly, that the educational endeavour which occupies and exhausts them could itself be rather absurd. The sensation subsides into an accusation that in his moment, or this instance, absurdity resides. Diminished accusations such as these reduce our discomfort. When encountered directly, the absurd is distinctly unsettling – all the better to confine it to this or that case of professional frustration. Hence for our most dogged and perceptive educational critics, a new benchmarking test, system of performance related pay, or fresh strategy for 'raising standards' is considered absurd, rather than the educational zeitgeist it may be symptomatic of.

*

Those seeking an encounter with the absurd may turn from Nietzsche to his absurd successor, Camus. Written with 'blistered and stiffened fingers',[29] Camus' wartime book *The Myth of Sisyphus* was an attempt to write 'without the aid of eternal values which, temporarily perhaps' were 'absent or distorted'.[30] Facing European disaster, this book was an invitation to embrace the absurd, to 'live and to create, in the very midst of the desert'.[31]

*

In our century the landscape remains obscene. Advanced nihilism and its pessimistic outlook afflict us too. Only, the affliction is differently felt. The old twentieth century fear of military annihilation and complete repression to the point of extinction, has been replaced by a more abstract, yet deeply persistent fear of impending civil and ecological collapse, a prospect rehearsed repeatedly in film. Our response is as abstract and edgeless as its foe is conceived. We late modern descendants of liberalism are distinguished by our reflexive impotence. We combine the weak cynicism of those who have 'seen it all', with the performative optimism and good cheer of those who can no longer be disappointed. Nowhere is this more evident than in education. It introduces us to the world and its realities, not so that we might better reject it, but as preparation to endure. We aspire to making things a little better about the edges.

*

Though Cynic perversion is almost beyond revival – being too readily recuperated by capital, diminished and pathologised – the mode of interruption offered by Cynicism is urgently missed today. It would attempt the absurd. Following Camus, the absurd offers potential for a more self-conscious mode of interruption that resists recuperation. It is represented by that scandalous figure, the absurd hero, who takes form in the closing pages of Camus' wartime novel, *The Outsider*.[32] Having spent the first half of the novel in a stupor, experiencing the world as a sequence of sensations, the absurd hero comes into being during the second half when forced to reflect on his existence.[33] Compelled by imprisonment and trial, this character begins to feel the burden of history and of the society in which he finds himself. Eventually he is sentenced to death. The decisive moment in condemning the absurd man, in deciding his crime is pre-meditated and fully conscious, is that moment where the prosecutor claims that here, before the jury, 'is an educated man'.[34] In this context education is no excuse. It is sufficient ground for conviction... The absurd educator faces the prospect of similar disapproval. This educator is castigated for being both absurd and educated – where the latter mark of distinction is used to condemn the former attitude. To be educated and absurd is inexcusable, or so it goes. But as the absurd educator is condemned, she nevertheless escapes the stupor of educational busy-work. Facing the judgement of her peers she is forced to reflect, and finds herself similarly burdened by history, and by the society in which she lives. She is tempted to abandon her absurd position, being susceptible to the old metaphysical promise. Yet along with the absurd hero who refuses to find solace in hope, or in his newfound facility for reflection,[35] who eventually lays his heart open to what he perceives to be "the benign indifference of the universe"[36] – the absurd educator does not find solace in the hope of redemption, or the securities of critique. She endures the heavy realisation that education could be nothing but a futile distraction, which promises and defers, and defers and promises.

*

Despite its allure for the educated nihilist, as concept and experience, the absurd has lost traction.[37] Camus made reference to the absurd in a way we no longer can. In *The Myth of Sisyphus* he took the absurd as his starting point, invoking 'an absurd sensitivity', which, he claimed, was commonly felt at the time.[38] The absurd feeling Camus found so abundant was the product of a collision between passionate belief and sore disappointment.[39] It was no accident that the absurd became the talk of the sixties, only to become a dulled and increasingly rare sensitivity in our more cynical present.

*

The world is not absurd in itself. Rather, the absurd is made present to us, through us. It is produced by how we position ourselves in relation to the universe. The absurd is a disease of the intellect bred to revere higher things, an intellect that expects the universe to mirror its ideas of justice and reason.

Absurd Lessons

'If man realized that the universe like him can love and suffer, he would be reconciled'.[40] If thought discovered its principles perfectly mirrored in phenomena, it would give birth on behalf of its originating thinker to 'an intellectual joy of which the myth of the blessed would be but a ridiculous imitation'.[41] Those who insist that life be meaningful would finally, and conclusively, find themselves vindicated. Alas, their story (a story which is yours and mine) is one of continual disappointment. We continue to live by ideals that, were they put to the test, would upset everything we believe. Those of us professing a secular outlook know the universe is indifferent to human suffering, and yet continue to act as if we were the exception. That all human toil and torment could be without reason and ultimately in vain is personally inconceivable; or to adopt different idiom, the very idea is so inhumanly grotesque it is beyond belief. And so, a hiatus is maintained between the acknowledged indifference of the universe, and the belief that humans are meaningful animals in control of their destiny, existing outside or against a reality in which entropy reigns supreme. This is how we position ourselves. This act of positioning defines us as absurd beings.

*

'This world in itself is not reasonable, that is all that can be said'.[42] It only becomes absurd through human contact. The absurd is generated where the need for understanding encounters the 'unreasonable silence of the world',[43] between 'the mind that desires and the world that disappoints', between our 'nostalgia for unity' and 'this fragmented universe'.[44] It appears precisely in this divorce, where irrational reality meets the 'wild longing for clarity' whose call has echoed in the human heart[45] since

Socrates, as Nietzsche would have it. Absurdity binds this desire to its impossible context 'as only hatred can weld two creatures together'.[46] It is a hostile, painful encounter, which education attempts to cover up with hopeful assurances.

*

Those seeking a direct encounter with the absurd consider hope to be a 'fatal evasion'[47] on par with suicide. For hope, like suicide,[48] is symptomatic of those who cannot endure an absurd existence. Undoubtedly, even just a little hope affords a consolation that few, if any, are able to resist. A declared passion for life is similarly evasive. It represents a retreat from the metaphysics of hope, a determined but reactive effort to find solace in 'what is'. A passion for education, also reactive, occurs where the value of education wears thin. A passion for education is indiscriminate in its attachments and not a little desperate. It is the response of those facing the loss of an object to which they have been long attached.

*

Properly felt, the absurd is not an abstract concept. It is something we attempt to live with in close proximity. In education the absurd is particularly hard to confront, despite longstanding disparity between our highest educational ideals and the unremittingly grubby nature of educational realities that remain subservient to relations of power, class and capital. This disparity perfectly exemplifies what Camus might describe as the presence of the absurd in education.[49] By profession, educators are protected from such encounters, somehow believing that despite it all, education can escape its grasp.

*

Assuming the absurd can still be experienced in an age of mass cynicism, it is hard to imagine how any educator who approaches the absurd could return to her profession. This educated nihilist would be left unable to operate, or could only continue on the condition the performative optimism of the profession were all the more doggedly embraced. This educated nihilist would return to work more devotional in her commitments than ever, clinging more tightly to a narrative of educational redemption, grasping with bloodless hands at old and tired assurances that education must, somehow, somewhere, have a core worth rescuing. Or she would quit.

*

The absurd brings painful ambivalence to those who can endure it. There is no either or. In this respect it affords a distinct opportunity for the educated nihilist, one that is difficult to grasp, admittedly. Nihilism must not entail, as its detractors would have it, that one gives up on everything with absolute severity. Another, less hopeful, more absurd education is imaginable, one in which absurdly-honest educators openly demonstrate how they are only pretending to knowledge with its attendant prestige, and absurdly-perceptive students do everything necessary to see through the pretence.[50] This breaks with mass cynicism. Pain is acknowledged. Melancholia subsides. Action ensues.

*

'To an absurd mind reason is useless and there is nothing beyond reason'.[51] Each rationality has its order and field of influence within which it is efficacious. That much can be admitted. But rationality on its own has no existence or global purchase. Like those who put their faith in reason, those who would scorn reason and admit the irrational, clearly have little stamina for the absurd. When it comes to reason they refuse ambivalence, insisting it be nothing or all.

*

'The absurd has meaning only in so far as it is not agreed to'.[52] As we approach it we are repelled. In it we find manifested 'this desire for unity, this longing to solve, this need for clarity and cohesion' combined with the clear 'impossibility of reducing this world to a rational and reasonable principle'. Calling back to us from its 'dizzying crest'[53] the absurd man shouts above the clamour of our hopes and makes an absurd promise: It is indeed possible 'to live *without appeal*'.[54] To which we reply: Is it also possible to *educate* without appeal? But the absurd man will prove nothing through reason. All notions of proof are given wide birth with one exception: Through action alone 'he gives proof of his only truth which is defiance'.[55]

*

'The absurd does not liberate; it binds'.[56] Its first and most perfect casualty found himself condemned to roll a huge bolder uphill, only to see his burden roll back to its starting point. Upon which the task of pushing upwards resumed. Chained to perpetual toil without consolation or hope, engaged in labour that had no ultimate value or meaning, possessed of its own closed and relentless logic, King Sisyphus, craftiest of men, became superior to his absurd task by embracing it.

*

'There is no fate that cannot be surmounted by scorn'.[57] From the mythical figure of Sisyphus to the everyday worker, Camus locates the absurd in that moment of absurd recognition. With rasping breath and a pained expression, the absurd man sees his plight for what it is. Following recognition, the challenge for Camus, and for us, is to engage in persistent rebellion, in a kind of revolt that has no definite future or resolution. Our revolt unfolds without giving in to hope or despair, without seeking consolation in higher things or declaring that everything is meaningless. But we are also told that the absurd man may look and act like any other. With Camus we discover that the absurd civil servant would look like the common civil servant; the absurd commuter like the common commuter. As such, each rebellion risks becoming little but a supercilious gaze, an expression of scorn, or a hidden contempt. The absurd gaze risks becoming defined by its reactive and weak hostility if not by its outright *ressentiment*.[58] At this point the Cynical educator draws away in disgust. Here absurd educator and absurd man part company. After all, educators have long carried the burden of that ancient commitment; to teach by example. The absurd educator – who for good or ill embodies her lesson – will look very different, and will appear in explicit contrast to the rest of her profession. Hers is not a supercilious gaze. The absurd educator conveys her experience of the absurd to others. Hers is an education without hope, but in rebellion.

*

The absurd is largely absent from view and recalled with difficulty. As more ambitious commitments to progressive educational ideals gave way to a vaguely felt romantic impulse, as mass cynicism extended its grip, the necessary conditions for absurd perception fell away. Attempting to raise the tone of once noble sounds, contemporary educators claim over and again, absently but insistently: education is good and worthwhile. This jaded insistence has become a measure of their cynicism. Uttered in despair, this conviction will not confront the cause of its gloom, the fact education is failing, by design. Without this conflict, the absurd retreats from view.

*

'A man who has become conscious of the absurd is for ever bound to it' – here Camus is a trifle optimistic.[59] But for the Cynic this remains true. Painful ambiguities are all we have left, the Cynic decides. An urban stray yet capable of faithful devotion, even discipline; a rogue with a beastly tongue but a heterodox moralist too. Who better to pursue, express and endure the absurdity of civilized living? Our Cynic survives ambiguity not in spite of it, but in pursuit of it. Forget scatological acts; the affirmation of ambiguity, its dogged embrace, is sufficient now for embarrassment.

*

Despite the mass cynicism of their occupants, educational institutions are full of bombast. Our universities are forever now saving the world – with rhetoric. On occasion the Cynic might take such rhetoric at face value and pursue it in earnest. In a context where everyone knows but nobody admits they have been abandoned, or at least been leached of content, this Cynic would not act out ideals to reassert them. The absurd educator does not follow to the letter the rhetoric of her institution in an effort to shame that institution into alignment with its flatulent claims. When absurd educator and Cynic decide to embody educational rhetoric in all its impossible excess, they make painfully apparent forgotten conflicts between educational dreams and their inevitable disappointments. Flavour returns, we taste the absurd.

*

The Cynical educator seeks out painful experiences because they are repellent. It is better to live with the absurd and teach absurdly this educator decides, than live with and perpetuate consolations of hope and education, promises of reason and order. It is better to embrace the ambiguity of absurd existence and be torn by ambiguity, than reconcile oneself to it. Educational promises are avoided: they lead to fixed rebellion – a revolt constrained by its hopes – or they lead to immobility and despair. The absurd is uniquely valuable, if not essential to the Cynical educator. It prompts to perpetual revolution.

The Cynical Educator

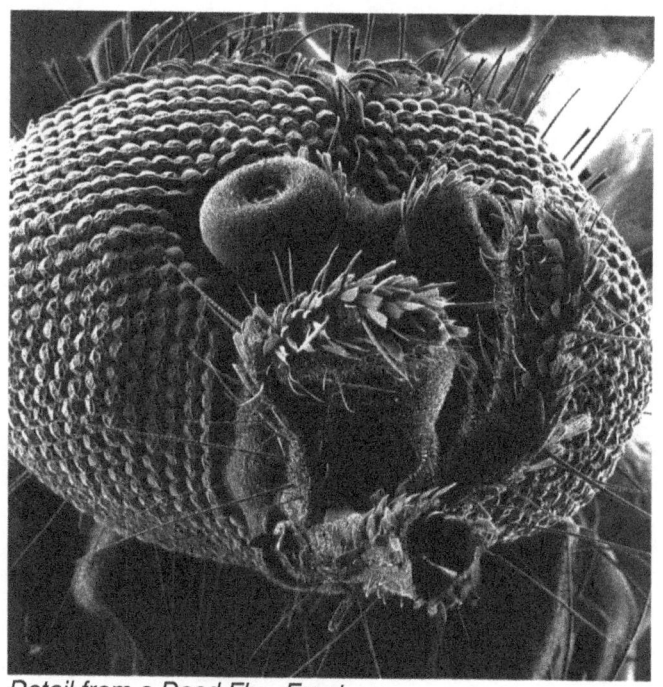

Detail from a Dead Fly - Front

NOTES

[1] This book was written with the aid of a fellowship from the Philosophy of Education Society of Great Britain. I am grateful to my editor, Christopher Land at Mayfly Books for supporting the project as well as my anonymous reviewers. The book is indebted to numerous conversations with colleagues and friends, including Emile Bojesen, Darren Webb, Kathryn Ecclestone, Wilfred Carr, Nick Peim, Tony Williams and Maurizio Toscano, as well as the close friendship and intellectual collaboration of Roy Goddard. I am particularly thankful to Sarah Spencer for her love, companionship, close reading and insight. This book is dedicated to our daughter, Sasha.

[2] Almost a century old, this refrain echoes in the ear of the educator (Wells, H. G. *The Outline of History: Being a Plain History of Life and Mankind.* London: Cassell, 1951 [1920]. p. 1192.). It recurs, for example, in *Stoner* a book recently become popular whose author – an English professor – described it upon retirement in 1985 as a book about teaching, about the sense of identity education gives the teacher, a book about teaching as a thing driven by love, by a commitment 'to keep the tradition going, because the tradition is civilisation' (Williams, John. *Stoner.* London: Vintage, 2012 [1965]. p. xi.): Here a love of teaching and literature is the love and salvation of civilisation.

[3] Some would have education reconceived, as study, for example, and thereby seem to escape a predicament where more education is the only remedy to educational problems. This is what Stefano Harney and Fred Moten argue in *The Undercommons* (Harney, Stefano and Moten, Fred. *The Undercommons: Fugitive Planning & Black Study.* Wivenhoe: Minor Compositions, 2013). Study is here conceptualised in opposition to institutionalised education. Study occurs inside and beyond its institutional sites, and is based on a questioning

of what mainstream education offers: 'what we want to do is to organize ourselves around the principle that we don't want everything they have. Not only is a lot of the shit that they have bad, but so too is their very mode of having' (ibid. p. 121). This invocation of study appears to think beyond education, and oppose itself to educational ways of having that are currently being 'farmed out' to others (ibid. p. 122). But this argument only works in a world where education does not already pervade society. Otherwise, an argument for study is an argument for more education. For study to release itself from education, it would need to confront that rather troubled individual, the educator within.

[4] Sloterdijk, Peter. *Critique of Cynical Reason*. Minneapolis: University of Minnesota Press, 2001 [1987].

[5] See: Osborne, Peter. Disguised as a dog. *Radical Philosophy* 2012; 174 (July/August). During the 1960s, and following their most violently indecent performances, Viennese Actionists such as Günter Brus were either incarcerated or fled the country. Unlike Diogenes, they did not 'remain in Athens' so to speak. Note too that between camera and audience the former takes precedence, where the latter is used to stage the former, performing a vital role in the composition of the photograph. For the Cynic, by contrast, the immediate audience takes precedence. See: Widrich, Mechtild. The Informative Public of Performance: A Study of Viennese Actionism, 1965-1970. *The Drama Review* 2013; 57(1).

[6] Recall Swift's parable of the spider and the bee in 'The Battle of the Books': Swift, Jonathan. *A Tale of a Tub and Other Works*. Oxford: Oxford University Press, 1704 [2008]. p. 113.

[7] Nietzsche, Friedrich. *Anti-Education: On the Future of Our Educational Institutions*. New York: New York Review Books, 2016 [1872]. p. 81.

[8] See, for example: Postman, Neil. *The End of Education: Redefining the Value of School*. New York: Vintage, 1996.

[9] A Dionysian wake would not announce a simple escape from all that is measured and restraining. As readers of *The Birth of Tragedy* may recall, Dionysian excess only appears by contrast

to Apolline restraint: 'the fact that he *appears* with this precision and clarity is the effect of Apollo' (Nietzsche, Friedrich. *The Birth of Tragedy*. London: Penguin, 2003 [1872]. §10).

[10] Sebald, W. G. *Austerlitz*. London: Penguin, 2002. p. 31.

[11] Hadot, Pierre. *Plotinus or The Simplicity of Vision*. Chicago: University of Chicago Press, 1998 [1989]. p. 17.

[12] Shit Academics Say, Twitter post, 26 October 2015, https://twitter.com/AcademicsSay.

[13] Another note, I know: Once endnotes reach a certain frequency they make themselves increasingly redundant.

[14] Shea, Louisa. *The Cynic Enlightenment: Diogenes in the Salon*. Baltimore: Johns Hopkins University Press, 2010. pp. 4-7.

[15] Foucault, Michel. On the Genealogy of Ethics: An Overview of Work in Progress. In: Rabinow, editor. *Essential Works of Foucault 1954-1984. Volume 1*. London: Penguin, 2000 [1983]. p. 256.

[16] Vattimo, Gianni. *The End of Modernity: Nihilism and Hermeneutics in Post-modern Culture*. Cambridge: Polity, 2002 [1988]. p. 13.

[17] Doeuff, Michèle Le. *Hipparchia's Choice*. New York: Columbia University Press, 2007 [1989]. p. 18.

[18] Doeuff. *Hipparchia's Choice*. p. 24.

[19] MacIntyre, Alasdair. The relationship of philosophy to its past. In: Rorty, Schneewind and Skinner, editors. *Philosophy in History: Essays in the historiography of philosophy*. Cambridge: Cambridge University Press, 1984. p. 32.

[20] Adlam, John. Going spiral? Phenomena of 'half-knowledge' in the experimental large group as temporary learning community. *Pedagogy, Culture & Society* 2014; 22(1). p. 158.

[21] Scanlon, Christopher. 'Defacing the Currency?': A Group-Analytic Appreciation of Homelessness, Dangerousness, Disorder and Other Inarticulate Speech of the Heart. *Group Analysis* 2011; 44(2). Adlam, John and Scanlon, Christopher. Personality Disorder and Homelessness: Membership and

'Unhoused Minds' in Forensic Settings. *Group Analysis* 2005; 38(3).

[22] Nietzsche, Friedrich. *The Gay Science: With a Prelude in Rhymes and an Appendix of Songs.* New York: Vintage, 1974 [1882]. §86.

[23] Nietzsche, Friedrich. *Daybreak: Thoughts on the prejudices of morality.* Cambridge: Cambridge University Press, 1997 [1881]. §117.

[24] Shea. *The Cynic Enlightenment.* p. 200.

II. Promised Goods

[1] Marx, Karl. *Capital: Volume I.* London: Penguin, 1990 [1867]. p. 103.

[2] Nietzsche, Friedrich. *The Will to Power.* New York: Vintage, 1968.

[3] Vonnegut, Kurt. Playboy Interview. *Wampeters, Foma & Granfalloons.* London: Granada, 1982 [1973]. p. 230.

[4] By way of an aside, one might argue it is here that Nietzsche comes closest to the Cynic position he appears to admire, where seriocomic laughter makes its mischief by revealing the comedy of our existence. See: Bracht Branham, R. Nietzsche's Cynicism: Uppercase or lowercase? In: Bishop, editor. *Nietzsche and Antiquity.* New York: Camden House, 2004.

[5] Heidegger, Martin. Nietzsche's Word: 'God Is Dead'. In: Young and Haynes, editors. *Off the Beaten Track.* Cambridge: Cambridge University Press, 2002 [1943]. p. 160.

[6] Vattimo. *The End of Modernity.* p. 19.

[7] Vattimo. *The End of Modernity.* p. 166.

[8] Nietzsche, Friedrich. *Thus Spoke Zarathustra: A Book for All and None.* Edinburgh: T. N. Foulis, 1909 [1883]. p. 255.

[9] Here I have in mind the Renaissance and later Romantic consumptive (more later) where consumption was, for a time, the desirable, and then fashionable disease of a social elite, before, long before it became associated with poverty and

degeneration. See: Arnold, Marc. *Disease, Class and Social Change: Tuberculosis in Folkestone and Sandgate, 1880-1930.* Newcastle upon Tyne: Cambridge Scholars Publishing, 2012.

[10] Nietzsche, Friedrich. The Anti-Christ. *Twilight of the Idols and The Anti-Christ.* London: Penguin, 2003 [1895]. §23.

[11] Heidegger. *Nietzsche's Word: 'God Is Dead'.* p. 166.

[12] Vattimo. *The End of Modernity.* p. 2.

[13] Nietzsche. *Daybreak.* §44.

[14] Foucault, Michel. *The Order of Things: An archaeology of the human sciences.* London: Tavistock, 1966 [1985]. p. 330.

[15] Vattimo. *The End of Modernity.* pp. 7-8.

[16] Vattimo. *The End of Modernity.* p. 169.

[17] Vattimo. *The End of Modernity.* p. 23.

[18] Plato. The Apology. *The Last Days of Socrates.* London: Penguin, 1993. 31d.

[19] Hadot, Pierre. *What is Ancient Philosophy?* Cambridge, Massachusetts: Harvard, 2004 [1995]. p. 34.

[20] Plato cited in Hadot, Pierre. *Philosophy as a Way of Life.* Oxford: Blackwell, 1987 [1995]. p. 95. This is Hadot's translation from Plato's *Meno*, 75c-d.

[21] Practiced here is the Socratic 'art of seducing souls...towards conversion' (Hadot. *Philosophy as a Way of Life.* p. 92-3).

[22] Hadot. *Plotinus or The Simplicity of Vision.*

[23] Hadot makes a distinction in this regard between teaching concerned with technical matters versus teaching concerned with existential questions: Building on this division, we might say that education today is predominantly concerned with 'everything that is technical'. It is concerned with things which can be dealt with more or less directly, having long given up on 'everything that touches the domain of the existential', on everything which remains ineffable and can only be alluded to indirectly. To qualify as educational concerns, these existential matters (how we respond to the inevitability of death, for example) must be translated into technical terms, which can be

dealt with and taught in a more straightforward manner (Hadot. *Philosophy as a Way of Life*. p. 285).

[24] Nietzsche, Friedrich. *Human, All Too Human*. London: Penguin, 2004 [1878]. §40.

[25] Carr, Wilfred and Kemmis, Stephen. *Becoming Critical: Education, Knowledge and Action Research*: Deakin University Press, 1986. p. 33.

[26] Carr, Wilfred. Educational Research as a practical science. *International Journal of Research & Method in Education* 2007; 30(3). p. 276.

[27] Gadamer, Hans-Georg. *Truth and Method*. London: Continuum, 2004 [1975]. p. 312.

[28] Carr and Kemmis. *Becoming Critical*. p. 33.

[29] Education has become the passionate attachment of the romantic educator, the heartfelt commitment of the modern educator who labours in and against a technocratic regime. Modern educational practice may remain haunted by praxis, but can ignore its basic principles, including many of those cited above. It forgets, too, the Aristotelian argument that 'a person who is overwhelmed by his passions suddenly no longer sees what is right to do in a given situation'. He loses mastery of himself and lets his passions decide what is right (Gadamer. *Truth and Method*. p. 319). Praxis remains, for Aristotle, a resolutely calculative activity, though its algorithms are of the moment.

[30] Gadamer. *Truth and Method*. p. 311.

[31] Gadamer. *Truth and Method*. p. 311.

[32] Gadamer. *Truth and Method*. p. 310.

[33] Cavarero, Adriana. *In Spite of Plato: A Feminist Rewriting of Ancient Philosophy*. Cambridge: Polity, 1995. p. 35.

[34] Cavarero. *In Spite of Plato*. p. 49.

[35] Plato. *Phaedo*. 64a-b.

[36] Plato. *Phaedo*. 64c.

[37] Plato. *Phaedo*. 65a.

[38] Plato. *Phaedo*. 67e.

Notes

[39] Plato. *Phaedo*. 68b.

[40] Hadot. *Philosophy as a Way of Life*. p. 96.

[41] To clarify, Platonic philosophers did not directly court death but learned to live in this world as if already dead. This notion preoccupied them for centuries, and so we have a philosopher such as Plotinus toiling away under its influence more than six hundred years later. For Plotinus, supreme transcendence was a spiritual state that the most practiced philosopher would only experience a handful of times. And so, each fleeting moment of ascent whereby the soul is lifted into the highest realms, would be accompanied by an inevitable descent. The problem the philosopher faced was that of reconciling these transitory and divine experiences with his more common, corporeal existence from which he now felt alienated. The philosopher had to 'learn to live, after contemplation', putting up with day-to-day life, making do with the quotidian (Hadot. *Plotinus or The Simplicity of Vision*. p. 65). For Plotinus, there was nothing wrong with material things, and the body itself was not inherently bad. The issue with the body, rather, was its 'excessive vitality' which served as a distraction (ibid. p. 81). The challenge was to overcome all such diversions and orient oneself towards that which is immaterial. The philosopher was not so much rejecting material reality here, as becoming preoccupied with a non-material transcendent state of existence. This was a question of preparing the soul for its next ascent, for which we must 'detach ourselves from life down here', becoming entirely passive in our contemplations, so that we are 'ready to receive the divine presence, when it manifests again' (ibid. p. 65). The soul must purify itself, removing all that is superfluous to this objective. Terrestrial things simply become irrelevant, and are to be disregarded so that the soul is ready to rise up and experience the ecstasy of transcendence. This realm lies far beyond the boundaries of individual personhood, and so with Plotinus we arrive at 'the only desire which defines him: no longer to be Plotinus' (ibid. p. 22). Believing our existence on earth to be only a shadow and a poor imitation of the world above, the philosopher attempts to live increasingly in that other world at

the expense of this one, which becomes as hollow and devoid of passion as his engagement with it.

Platonism was not the only school to extend its influence into late antiquity, nor was its influence unadulterated. This was a period in which philosophers and philosophical agendas were often alloyed to one another. The educational, philosophical legacies were mixed as were their originating traditions:

The dogmas of these other Athenian schools varied considerably. On one point however, there was broad agreement. Following Socrates, it was axiomatic that ignorance must be challenged. Hence, all that was done in the name of education could now be justified by this commitment to fight ignorance, since ignorance was associated with all that is wretched in human existence. Each school in classical antiquity had its own solution to the problem of ignorance, and this proffered solution became its definition of generosity. Each defined an educational path that would lead its beneficiaries to see the world differently. This would entail a radical adjustment to one's 'entire way of thinking and being', which not only changed how one viewed and evaluated the world, but how one lived in it too (Hadot. *What is Ancient Philosophy?* p. 102). The educational fight against ignorance varied according to how its chief evils were defined. The Epicureans sought to educate desire, claiming that we suffer so much because we are ignorant of the conditions required for genuine pleasure. We are haunted by insatiable desires and hopes that corrupt our ability to enjoy. Genuine pleasure is a simple thing, which can arrive once the body is freed of hunger, thirst and cold on the one hand, and unnecessary desire on the other. The Epicurean recites: 'Thanks be to blessed Nature, who has made necessary things easy to obtain, and who has made things difficult to obtain unnecessary'. This meditative philosophy 'consists in limiting one's appetites – suppressing those desires which are neither natural nor necessary, and limiting as much as possible those which are natural but not necessary' where the latter are dangerous, since they 'may result in violent and excessive passions' (ibid. p. 117). The Epicurean tradition reserves the right, of course, to define which desires are allowed, and which are to be avoided. The Epicurean's desires were to be developed and denied in seclusion, with masters and disciples working together to cure their souls. Epicurus himself assumed first in person, and later through writing, the role of a 'director of conscience' (ibid. p. 123). Members of his school were encouraged to act 'as though Epicurus were watching you' (Seneca cited in ibid. p. 124). Epicureans would also watch over one other, training their inclinations through exercises in the 'examination of one's conscience, confession, and fraternal correction' (ibid. p. 124), wherein masters would hand out reproaches, and disciples would volunteer their faults. In short, the serenity, if not repose, to which each member aspired was underwritten by a shared discipline of restraint and denial. [By way of an aside, we might note how the Epicurean school developed confessional practices that were almost proto-Christian in their attempts to educate the conscience. At this point however, it is worth turning to Foucault who was careful to distinguish Christian confessional practices from their Greek and Roman precursors. Foucault argues that Epicurean practices were designed to reorient the subject's being, without taking 'the soul or the self as the real object of knowledge' (Foucault, Michel. *The Hermeneutics of the Subject: Lectures at the Collège de France 1981-1982.* Basingstoke: Palgrave Macmillan, 2005 [1982]. p. 243). The subject was not expected to 'tell the truth about himself' and hence reveal the workings of his soul as in later Christian practices; rather, subjects were encouraged to relate to themselves and the world differently, or so the argument goes, without the imperative to divulge a 'true self' (Foucault, Michel. *On the Government of the Living: Lectures at the Collège de France 1979-1980.* Basingstoke: Palgrave Macmillan, 2014 [1980]. p. 321).

The Stoics followed a very different path believing that happiness consists not in a redefinition of pleasure, but in one's alignment to the 'good'. Unlike the Platonic tradition, for which the good is a worthy target but is ultimately unrealisable in this life (with all its bodily distractions), Stoicism claimed the good to be attainable through a careful cultivation of the self. It was resolutely materialist in this respect, seeking not to deny the body in favour of a transcendental realm, but to reconcile the body to its material existence. This attention to its material existence was still a denial of the body, however. Rejecting Plato's conception of the Forms, Seneca, for example, nevertheless viewed the body from above, as 'nothing more or less than a fetter on my freedom'. Harassed by 'the body's overwhelming weight, the soul is in captivity unless philosophy comes to its rescue, bidding it breathe more freely' in the contemplation of things far above (Seneca. *Letters from a Stoic*. London: Penguin, 2004. p. 122). Equally, Seneca denies the body in his meditation upon death, where he recommends that we make death 'actual in life' by living each day as if it were our last (Foucault. *The Hermeneutics of the Subject*. p. 504). Every day 'should be regulated as if it were the one that brings up the rear, the one that rounds out and completes our lives' (Seneca. *Letters from a Stoic*. p. 58). Those who practise this meditation should eventually be able to go to sleep and contemplate death with contentment, declaring: 'I have lived' (ibid. p. 59). Living each day as if it were one's last does not imply for the Stoic that one lives that day to the full. Rather, thinking from the perspective of one's imminent death is designed to 'immobilize the present', forcing one to take an instantaneous view of it from above (Foucault. *The Hermeneutics of the Subject*. p. 479). Believing each current moment to potentially represent what one was doing when one died, causes one to reflect upon its value with greater attention. Hence the Stoic asks: What would I like to be doing the moment I die? What would it say about my life? If I can think of something better or more worthwhile, perhaps I should be doing that instead, if this moment is to be my last? Consequently, the Stoic is encouraged to inspect each moment for its moral value. By focusing so intently on what one can influence, the Stoic was expected to face everything beyond our control with self-composure, responding to all misfortunes, including one's inevitable death with a resigned yet cheerful shrug. Human existence will always be, in part, a tragic affair buffeted by causes beyond our control. Hence, the Stoic practiced a form of determined acquiescence to the accidents and setbacks that life throws up, to be combined with a deliberate focus on the only thing remaining that is within our control, this being our personal commitment to what is good.

Hence the Stoic must both confront one's fate and even one's death with radical indifference, whilst pursuing that which one considers morally right. Stoicism offers a way of coping with existence by dulling its adverse effects. Unlike the Epicureans who sought to detach thought from all things painful and focus instead on attainable pleasures, the Stoics focused resolutely on all possible misfortunes, seeking to picture every conceivable disaster in advance so that they would be fully prepared to bear adversity when it arrived. Where the Epicureans sought to relax the soul, the Stoics taught it to 'stretch itself tight' (Hadot. *Philosophy as a Way of Life.* p. 88). Buttressed in this way, it would become impregnable. The point was to build and then occupy an 'inner citadel' from which one views the world from above and with a uniformly benign gaze (see: Hadot, Pierre. *The Inner Citadel: The Meditations of Marcus Aurelius.* Cambridge, Massachusetts: Harvard University Press, 2001). Stoicism insists on noticing 'the puniness of human beings, lost in the cosmos'. We are to become reconciled to our puniness, the Stoic decides, though in a way that allows the Stoic to pursue undistracted the 'transcendence of [his own] moral conscience' (ibid. p. 311). This transcendent view takes years to cultivate, as the Stoic learns to become indifferent to all things produced by external causes. Unaffected by external forces, through a 'discipline of assent' (ibid. p. 101) that refuses to pass judgement on material matters which are neither good nor bad in themselves, the Stoic is free to cultivate himself. This is the philosophy of the emperor, or statesman, who decides that he has no time or patience to constantly second-guess the meaning of worldly things, deciding instead to deal with matters according to the facts of their appearance. The world is brutal, he decides, but we should not regret that fact, and decide that it is a 'bad' state of affairs to be constantly deplored. Free of such false judgements – 'things simply are as they are, they are not good or bad in themselves' – the Stoic is at liberty to lavish attention on the only project worth pursuing, his own singular 'goodness'. It would be a lifelong pursuit.

The Sceptics sought peace of mind by more radical means. Believing all human judgements to be in error, and hence the source of all human misery, the Sceptics sought to suspend judgement entirely. They could not cope with the existence of such widespread ignorance, and so attempted to step over it, and hence over all human understanding, as one steps over something dirty in the street. The Sceptic would live like everyone else, existing from day to day, conforming to custom, obeying social convention, satisfying natural desires. This would be a return to 'simplicity'. Philosophy would be employed as a purgative, used to evacuate all higher notions and forms including philosophy itself. With one's judgement suspended, no single event in one's life could be considered better than any other, and so the Sceptic would face life, and everything it throws up with equanimity.

Despite obvious variations between each philosophical school, they shared a common educational point of view. Each school recommended its own system of life-denial, connecting its regimen to a decidedly abstract notion of the philosophical, and hence educational good that would be served through one's obedience to its precepts. Each philosophy insisted on a kind of deferral, which can be explained across schools by reference to the idea of wisdom or *sophia,* that was at their root. Conceptions of wisdom varied widely of course, as did recommendations for how one might best work towards it.

[42] Hadot. *What is Ancient Philosophy?* p. 4.

[43] This argument concerning wisdom is not without controversy. It draws from the work of Pierre Hadot, in which it is claimed that ancient philosophy is best understood as a series of spiritual exercises. Philosophy, here defined as the 'love of and search for wisdom', entailed for each philosophical school a certain way of life for which wisdom was a guiding ideal (Hadot. *What is Ancient Philosophy?* p. 102). In Hadot's interpretation of the *Symposium,* for example, it is argued that 'philosophy is not wisdom, but a way of life and discourse determined by the idea of wisdom' (ibid. p. 46). This, for Hadot, is part of the 'grandeur and the paradox of ancient philosophy' in that it is 'at one and the same time, conscious of the fact that wisdom is inaccessible, and convinced of the necessity of pursuing spiritual progress' (Hadot. *Philosophy as a Way of Life.* p. 265). It is notable that Foucault drew attention to a similar point of

distinction, claiming that the ancient and contrasting figure of the sage achieves wisdom through inspiration rather than reason, though 'nothing obliges him to share his wisdom, to teach it, or demonstrate it' (Foucault, Michel. *The Courage of Truth: Lectures at the Collège de France 1983-1984*. Basingstoke: Palgrave Macmillan, 2011 [1984]. p. 17). By contrast, the philosopher-teacher is always on the path approaching wisdom, and unlike the sage, experiences the obligation to teach, an office filled most famously by Socrates. Against the sage whose wisdom is distant and reserved, the philosopher-teacher's wisdom is applied, directed to individuals and situations in an attempt, however faltering, to assist the philosopher's interlocutors to live a better life (ibid.).

[44] See: Hadot. *What is Ancient Philosophy?* p. 47.

[45] Hadot. *What is Ancient Philosophy?* p. 102.

[46] Hadot. *What is Ancient Philosophy?* p. 13.

[47] See, for example: Quinn, Josephine Crawley and Brooke, Christopher. 'Affection in Education': Edward Carpenter, John Addington Symonds and the politics of Greek love. *Oxford Review of Education* 2011; 37(5).

[48] Cavarero cited in: Clack, Beverley. *Sex and Death: A Reappraisal of Human Mortality*. Cambridge: Polity, 2002. p. 15.

[49] Clifford, Geraldine J. *Those Good Gertrudes: A Social History of Women Teachers in America*. Baltimore: Johns Hopkins University Press, 2014.

[50] Walkerdine, Valerie and Lucey, Helen. *Democracy in the Kitchen: Regulating Mothers and Socialising Daughters*. London: Virago, 1989.

[51] Skeggs, Beverly. *Formations of Class & Gender: Becoming Respectable*. London: Sage, 1997.

[52] Against this 'noble' lineage of educated men there is a perspective that does not view death as if it were an argument against life. Death must not be treated as a sign of the futility of life. Equally, death must not signify the ultimate boundary separating this dirty, perishable world from an eternal realm of philosophical thought. There is a conception of death that does

not support metaphysics. There is a conception that recognises death as birth, death as productive of other transient things. This would be a death to be affirmed. As Cavarero argues, this would be a conception of a 'kind of death that is not yet placed in isolation at the centre, as though dismally supporting the obsession with metaphysics, but is linked to birth as to a living context of its own occurring'. This would be a Dionysian conception of death, 'where birth and death are but rhythm and cadence' (Cavarero. *In Spite of Plato*. p. 113.).

III. Benevolent Educators

[1] In the third century Plotinus was still able to man his classroom, perhaps separated by a curtain from the street, where pupils gathered to hear him and his disciples discoursing (see: Hadot. *Plotinus or The Simplicity of Vision*. p. 82.)

[2] Brown, Peter. *The World of Late Antiquity*. London: Thames & Hudson, 1971. p. 72.

[3] Foucault. *The Hermeneutics of the Subject*. pp. 136-44.

[4] A point made in: Foucault. *The Courage of Truth*. Foucault. *The Hermeneutics of the Subject*. pp. 372-80.

[5] Brown, Peter. *The Body and Society: Men, Women and Sexual Renunciation in Early Christianity. Twentieth-Anniversary Edition*. New York: Columbia University Press, 2008. p. 27.

[6] See: Brown. *The Body and Society*. p. 22.

[7] An early version of this technique can perhaps be observed in Philodemus – who studied at the Epicurean school in Athens before moving to Rome and occupying the position of private counsellor. He describes a way of binding educator to pupil, a technique involving a kind of parrhesia – a mode of truth telling involving, amongst other things, frank speech. In one recovered fragment, Philodemus explains that by speaking freely, the educator will intensify and enliven the student's benevolence. At first sight a rather peculiar suggestion, it makes greater sense when placed within the more general Epicurean emphasis on the importance of 'reciprocal friendship', where, leading by

example, the educator encourages students to speak freely, and thereby bind themselves to one another through their mutual confidences (see: Foucault. *The Hermeneutics of the Subject.* p. 389.). Outside the securities of that philosophical school, in a context where educational relationships could no longer appeal to the authority of masters of tradition passing down the wisdom of Epicurus, such reciprocal relationships would gain greater significance, basing themselves more explicitly within the promise of mutual salvation (see: ibid. pp. 390-1. See also: Foucault, Michel. *The Care of the Self.* London: Penguin, 1990 [1984]. p. 52.).

[8] See: Foucault. *The Hermeneutics of the Subject.* pp. 396-9.

[9] Galen. *On the passions and errors of the soul*: Ohio State University Press., 1963. p. 36.

[10] Galen. *On the passions and errors of the soul.* p. 33.

[11] Galen. *On the passions and errors of the soul.* p. 35.

[12] Galen. *On the passions and errors of the soul.* p. 34.

[13] Galen. *On the passions and errors of the soul.* p. 53.

[14] See: Brown. *The Body and Society.* p. 18.

[15] Galen. *On the passions and errors of the soul.* p. 59.

[16] Galen. *On the passions and errors of the soul.* p. 53.

[17] Galen. *On the passions and errors of the soul.* p. 56.

[18] In the first century, Emperor Nero's advisor, Seneca, devises a similar argument in favour of the educator's frank speech: again we find how the educator should be valued for saying things that at times one would not wish to hear, discoursing against anger, for example, or in favour of clemency. For the powerful, Seneca decides, mercy without pity is strength; anger without exception is weakness (Seneca. *Dialogues and Essays.* Oxford: Oxford University Press, 2007.). In an imperial system where force is routine, violence is systematic, slavery naturalised, and power guaranteed, the restraint of the aristocratic class becomes the apparent measure of its greatness. Unlike Galen, who believed that the position of the educator who teaches his patron to restrain his passions is best occupied by a stranger, Seneca suggests that the educator

must also be a friend (see: Foucault. *The Hermeneutics of the Subject*. pp. 400-7. And: Seneca. *Letters from a Stoic.*). In the second century, to take another example, Emperor Marcus Aurelius was taught by a sequence of social inferiors, each considered a mere epigone in his chosen tradition of Stoic philosophy. Not all teachers of Marcus Aurelius were personal tutors however. Apollonius of Chalcedon and Sextus of Chaeronea 'were professors in charge of a school', to whom Marcus was forced to travel in order to hear their lectures (Hadot. *The Inner Citadel*. p. 15). Indeed, it is said that Apollonius refused to come to the palace to give lessons to his royal student, declaring that: "The disciple must come to the master, and not the master to the disciple" (cited in ibid.). Evidently the ancient tradition of philosopher-sage, and the more recent tradition of philosopher-tutor, were concurrent at this point. Relations with his favourite teacher, a personal tutor called Junius Rusticus, were at times a little stormy, yet Marcus credits his teacher with not only reforming his character, but also for teaching him the virtue of indulgence, a virtue which Rusticus embodied each time Marcus became irascible. Marcus thereby testifies to the importance of a relationship of tolerance between a student and his tutor, though now the argument is made from the perspective of the student (see: ibid. pp. 9-10.).

[19] Brown, Peter. *Power and Persuasion in Late Antiquity*. Madison: University of Wisconsin Press, 1992. p. 7.

[20] Brown. *Power and Persuasion in Late Antiquity*. p. 4.

[21] Brown. *Power and Persuasion in Late Antiquity*. pp. 30-1.

[22] Brown. *Power and Persuasion in Late Antiquity*. p. 50.

[23] Brown. *Power and Persuasion in Late Antiquity*. p. 52.

[24] Brown. *Power and Persuasion in Late Antiquity*. p. 55.

[25] Brown. *Power and Persuasion in Late Antiquity*. p. 56.

[26] Brown. *Power and Persuasion in Late Antiquity*. p. 123.

[27] The Roman empire, so it goes, had become a 'colossal bureaucratic apparatus' whose workings most individuals 'could not fathom or influence'. As its power to 'rouse feelings of citizenship and commitment to the state' dissipated, Roman

subjects sought meaning elsewhere. (Sloterdijk. *Critique of Cynical Reason*. pp. 170-1).

[28] Sloterdijk. *Critique of Cynical Reason*. p. 171.

[29] Brown. *The Body and Society*. p. 49.

[30] This was Anthony the Great. Dorotheus of Gaza said something similar: 'Let us pay attention to ourselves, my brothers, and let us be vigilant, while we still have time... Since the beginning of our conversation two or three hours have elapsed, and we have come closer to death; yet we see without fear that we are wasting our time' (both cited in Hadot. *What is Ancient Philosophy?* pp. 242-3.)

[31] Evagrius of Pontus cited in: Hadot. *What is Ancient Philosophy?* p. 246.

[32] Clement of Alexandria cited in: Brown. *The Body and Society*. p. 31.

[33] Dorotheus of Gaza cited in: Hadot. *What is Ancient Philosophy?* p. 245. Here, Hadot observes, was perhaps an echo of the Epicurean injunction: 'Do not seek to have that which happens happen as you wish. Wish that what happens may happen as it happens, and you will be happy' (ibid.).

[34] Brown. *The Body and Society*. p. 223.

[35] Clement of Alexandria cited in: Hadot. *What is Ancient Philosophy?* p. 246.

[36] This point is made by Brown (Brown. *The Body and Society*. p. 235.), who argues; whilst Christian ascetics may have given the body 'an almost oppressive prominence' as if 'motivated by hatred of the body', if we retrospectively focus only on such bodily denials we risk missing 'its most novel and its most poignant aspect', which was that the defiled body was also seen (as stated above) as the privileged training ground of the soul.

[37] 'Christianity is Platonism for the 'common people''. (Nietzsche, Friedrich. *Beyond Good and Evil: Prelude to a Philosophy of the Future*. Oxford: Oxford University Press, 1998 [1886]. p. 4.)

[38] Hadot. *What is Ancient Philosophy?* p. 252.

[39] According to one interpretation, the baptismal water was 'the water of death', the bath into which one was put, was 'Christ's tomb' (Foucault. *On the Government of the Living*. p. 156).

[40] Foucault. *On the Government of the Living*. p. 156.

[41] Foucault. *On the Government of the Living*. p. 105.

[42] Kelly, Henry Ansgar. *The Devil at Baptism: Ritual, Theology, and Drama*. Eugene, Oregon: Wipf & Stock Publishers, 2004 [1985]. pp. 126-7.

[43] Tertullian cited in: Foucault. *On the Government of the Living*. p. 117.

[44] See: Johnson, Maxwell E. *The Rites of Christian Initiation: Revised and Expanded Edition*. Collegeville, Minnesota: Liturgical Press, 2007. p. 97. At the end of the second century, practices of catechesis were becoming institutionalised. This can be seen in *The Apostolic Tradition*, an early third century text attributed to Hippolytus and considered to be one of the first clear accounts of early Christian baptismal ritual in the West (see: Kelly. *The Devil at Baptism*.). Its contents are nevertheless disputed, since the original text does not survive, leading scholars to question whether some of the practices described might date from the fourth century or later (see: Johnson. *The Rites of Christian Initiation*. pp. 101-10).

[45] Johnson. *The Rites of Christian Initiation*. p. 97. The exclusion of pagan teachers suggests a clear boundary at this point between secular teachers and Christian educators, presumably because the former taught the pagan arts (see: Cramer, Peter. *Baptism and Change in the Early Middle Ages, c. 200 - c. 1150*. Cambridge: Cambridge University Press, 1993. p. 16).

[46] Foucault. *On the Government of the Living*. p. 150.

[47] Foucault. *On the Government of the Living*. p. 151.

[48] This is from a fifth century text: 'If while the bishop pronounces this exorcism, anyone should become agitated and suddenly rise up and break into tears or shout, or foam at the mouth or gnash his teeth, or shamelessly stare about, or become excessively uplifted, or be seized by a sudden impulse and rush away' the candidate is put to one side, so that he can

be 'exorcized by the priests until he is cleansed, and then baptized' (cited in Kelly. *The Devil at Baptism*. p. 141.).

[49] Foucault. *On the Government of the Living*. p. 146.

[50] Kelly. *The Devil at Baptism*. p. 273.

[51] Cramer. *Baptism and Change in the Early Middle Ages*. p. 11.

[52] Augustine cited in: Kelly. *The Devil at Baptism*. p. 115.

[53] Foucault. *On the Government of the Living*. p. 153. Johnson. *The Rites of Christian Initiation*. p. 99.

[54] Hippolytus cited in Kelly. *The Devil at Baptism*. p. 84.

[55] Kelly. *The Devil at Baptism*. p. 88.

[56] Foucault. *On the Government of the Living*. p. 121.

[57] Original sin was not original to Christianity; theologians developed conceptions of it during late antiquity.

[58] Foucault. *On the Government of the Living*. p. 125.

[59] MacIntyre, Alasdair. *God, Philosophy, Universities. A Selective History of the Catholic Philosophical Tradition*. Plymouth: Rowman & Littlefield, 2009. p. 22.

[60] Foucault. *On the Government of the Living*. p. 125.

[61] MacIntyre. *God, Philosophy, Universities*. p. 25.

[62] Kelly, Henry Ansgar. *Satan: A Biography*. Cambridge: Cambridge University Press, 2006. p. 7.

[63] Foucault. *On the Government of the Living*. p. 125.

[64] Following baptism, the chief problem a Christian faced was that of falling back into sin and foregoing the promise of salvation. Life after baptism became a matter of avoiding relapse, or if it occurred; of redeeming the soul a second time. A second penance was devised for such cases, allowing those who had offended God to atone for their sins within a regimen that would also strengthen their ability to resist the devil. As an institutional procedure it rose to prominence during the persecutions of the third century, where baptised Christians were routinely forced to renounce their faith in an attempt to eradicate Christianity from the Roman Empire (Foucault. *On the Government of the Living*. p. 199). Like baptism, second

penance was a unique event, only becoming repeatable from the sixth and seventh centuries, whereupon it was divided into a whole sequence of individual penitential acts that could be observed in succession after each isolated sin (ibid. pp. 194-5). During second penance the sinner would join the order of penitents, remain within it for several years, and be remembered for the rest of his or her life as having been a penitent. Individual penitents were not expected to 'do this or that or to renounce this or that' in isolation – every aspect of their existence was at stake (ibid. p. 197). Again, as with baptism, the penitent was expected to manifest the truth of his or her soul, which was a first step towards taking responsibility for that soul, and its education. This manifestation did not at this point in the second and third century, involve a detailed confession of every sin committed. Rather, each penitent manifested the truth of the soul in more general terms, through collective prayer during which each penitent 'acknowledges before God and, consequently, before the others that he has sinned and is a sinner' (ibid. p. 203), or through ritual where the penitent would undergo a public act of supplication, pleading for entry at the door of the church, begging to be readmitted (see: ibid. pp. 205-8). This latter spectacle was, arguably, only the most exaggerated manifestation of a more 'permanent drama of repentance', during which the penitent would fast and otherwise seek out discomfort to manifest externally the conversion he or she was expected to be engaged with more or less constantly within (ibid. p. 210). The penitent was expected to relinquish his or her attachments to the world, overcome its distractions and temptations, once again hoping to guarantee rebirth and a future life by renouncing this life, seeking death and mortification for a life that was already fallen. The supplication of the penitent was, as Foucault put it, a matter of 'manifesting what one is and, at the same time, erasing what one is' (ibid. p. 214). Admission to the order of penitents – with its lifelong commitment to shame and supplication – was not guaranteed. Indeed, a whole procedure was devised to decide which of the fallen would be admitted. Accordingly, Foucault claims that this examination of the would-be penitent, was not, as in later monastic practice, an 'examination of conscience' designed to scrutinize the 'recesses of the heart' in order to divine if the candidate was sincere in his or her repentance. That remained a matter for God to decide (ibid. p. 200). Those judging admission could only guess at the commitment of the would-be penitent, though the framework of an incepting examination that served itself, but only to a limited extent, as a test of commitment. Crucially, however, penitents were not coopted by force, but were to consider their inclusion in the order as if it were a privilege bestowed upon them. Hence penitence was not inflicted upon unwilling subjects. Aspiring penitents were expected to desire wholeheartedly those practices of personal discomfort and public shame that penitence involved. Their commitment to the educational good promised by penitence, was a condition of entry.

[65] Foucault. *On the Government of the Living.* p. 126.

[66] Foucault. *On the Government of the Living.* p. 127.

[67] According to Brown, a whole succession of highly educated Christians ('master practitioners in Greek and Latin style') backed 'into the limelight that they had brought to bear on the illiterate monks, apostles, and martyrs' (Brown. *Power and Persuasion in Late Antiquity.* p. 74). Rather paradoxically, Christianity was able to mobilise the high culture of a Roman elite in terms comfortable to them, whilst asserting a religion which claimed at first to speak to the lowest members of society in their language.

[68] Brown. *The World of Late Antiquity.* p. 104.

[69] Smith, Katherine Allen. *War and the making of Medieval Monastic Culture.* Woodbridge: Boydell Press, 2011. p. 38.

[70] Smith. *War and the making of Medieval Monastic Culture.* pp. 89-96.

[71] Brown. *The World of Late Antiquity.* p. 110.

[72] Brown. *The Body and Society.* pp. xlv-xlvi.

[73] Brown. *The Body and Society.* p. xlvi.

[74] Brown. *The Body and Society.* p. 84.

[75] Brown (*The Body and Society.* p. 257.) argues that by the fifth century this radical stance had softened. The continence of monks was now seen as a mark of distinction, allowing them 'to

stand before the throne of God as the representatives of common humanity'.

[76] Brown. *The Body and Society*. p. 173.

[77] Foucault. *On the Government of the Living*. pp. 264-5.

[78] Foucault. *On the Government of the Living*. p. 266.

[79] Foucault. *On the Government of the Living*. pp. 267-9.

[80] The influential 'Rule of Saint Benedict', a book of precepts concerning monastic life, is attributed to Benedict of Nursia in the sixth century, who was heavily influenced by Cassian. It describes a monastic order run under the auspices of an abbot, a figure who is more a disciplinarian overlord than he is a spiritual guide. The abbot makes sure that the Rule is followed, that discipline is maintained. He is not a great philosopher or theologian who embodies the poise and virtue to which all aspire (see: Coon, Lynda L. *Dark Age Bodies: Gender and Monastic Practice in the Early Medieval West*. Philadelphia: University of Pennsylvania Press, 2011.).

[81] Coon. *Dark Age Bodies*. p. 76.

[82] Foucault. *On the Government of the Living*. p. 269.

[83] Ibid. pp. 269-70.

[84] Foucault, Michel. *Security, Territory, Population: Lectures at the Collège de France 1977-1978*. Basingstoke: Palgrave Macmillan, 2004 [1978]. p. 177.

[85] Foucault. *On the Government of the Living*. p. 271.

[86] Foucault. *On the Government of the Living*. p. 273.

[87] Foucault. *Security, Territory, Population*. p. 178.

[88] Foucault. *On the Government of the Living*. p. 291.

[89] Foucault. *On the Government of the Living*. p. 292.

[90] Foucault. *On the Government of the Living*. pp. 207-8.

[91] Brown. *The Body and Society*. p. 246.

[92] Foucault. *On the Government of the Living*. p. 306.

[93] Foucault. *On the Government of the Living*. p. 302.

[94] Foucault. *On the Government of the Living*. p. 306.

[95] Brown. *The Body and Society.* p. 231.

IV. Our Educational Conscience

[1] Seneca. *Letters from a Stoic.* p. 37.

[2] Seneca. *Letters from a Stoic.* pp. 37-8.

[3] Seneca. *Letters from a Stoic.* p. 37.

[4] Seneca. *Letters from a Stoic.* p. 38.

[5] Seneca. *Letters from a Stoic.* pp. 47-54.

[6] Seneca. On the Shortness of Life. *Dialogues and Essays.* Oxford: Oxford University Press, 2007. p. 142.

[7] Seneca. On the Shortness of Life. p. 155.

[8] Seneca. On the Shortness of Life. p. 141.

[9] Seneca. On the Shortness of Life. p. 157.

[10] Seneca. *Letters from a Stoic.* p. 53.

[11] Seneca. *Letters from a Stoic.* p. 60.

[12] Seneca. *Letters from a Stoic.* p.60.

[13] Seneca. *Letters from a Stoic.* p. 60.

[14] Seneca. *Letters from a Stoic.* p. 207.

[15] Seneca. *Letters from a Stoic.* pp. 151-61.

[16] Seneca. *Letters from a Stoic.* p. 212.

[17] Hunter, Ian. *Rethinking the school: Subjectivity, bureaucracy, criticism.* New York: St Martin's Press, 1994. p. xxi.

[18] Foucault. *Security, Territory, Population.* p. 125.

[19] Foucault. *Security, Territory, Population.* p. 126.

[20] Foucault. *Security, Territory, Population.* p. 127.

[21] Foucault. *Security, Territory, Population.* p. 128.

[22] Foucault. *Security, Territory, Population.* p. 128.

[23] Foucault. *Security, Territory, Population.* pp. 128-9.

[24] Foucault. *Security, Territory, Population.* p. 129.

[25] Foucault. *Security, Territory, Population.* p. 169.

[26] Foucault. *Security, Territory, Population.* p. 171.

[27] Foucault. *Security, Territory, Population.* p. 172.

[28] Foucault. *Security, Territory, Population.* p. 130.

[29] Hunter. *Rethinking the school.* pp. 85-6.

[30] Hunter. *Rethinking the school..* p. 168.

[31] Nietzsche. *The Anti-Christ.* §24.

[32] Nietzsche. *The Anti-Christ.* §51.

[33] Nietzsche. *The Anti-Christ.* §51.

[34] Foucault. *Security, Territory, Population.* p 181.

[35] Foucault. *Security, Territory, Population.* p. 182.

[36] Foucault. *Security, Territory, Population.* p. 183.

[37] Foucault. *Security, Territory, Population.* p. 182.

[38] Nietzsche. *The Anti-Christ.* §51.

[39] Nietzsche. *The Anti-Christ.* §14.

[40] Nietzsche. *The Anti-Christ.* §14.

[41] The Wars of Religion, the Reformation, and the Counter-Reformation can be viewed in this light, as battles over and concerning the pastorate. Its membership, for example, becomes a point of contention. Can parish priests be seen as pastors? 'Yes', said Wycliffe, following which 'a whole series of Protestant Churches will say yes, each in their way...' The Catholic Church 'will obstinately reply: No, parish priests are not pastors' – only bishops can hold this office (Foucault. *Security, Territory, Population.* p. 153). But Christianity had already laid claim over the government of men. The question became, which version of Christianity must dominate the fold.

[42] Foucault. *Security, Territory, Population.* p. 150.

[43] Nietzsche. *The Anti-Christ.* §38.

[44] Foucault. *Security, Territory, Population.* p. 148.

[45] Hunter. *Rethinking the school.* p. 1.

[46] Foucault. *Security, Territory, Population.* pp. 208-14.

[47] Foucault. *Security, Territory, Population.* p. 201.

[48] Nietzsche. *The Anti-Christ.* §61.

Notes

[49] Luther, Martin. To the Christian Nobility of the German Nation concerning the Reform of the Christian Estate. In: Tappert, editor. *Selected Writings of Martin Luther 1517-1520*. Philadelphia: Fortress Press, 1967 [1520]. p. 263.

[50] Luther. *To the Christian Nobility*. p. 260.

[51] Somewhat disavowed: Kinney, Daniel. Cynic Selfhood in Medieval and Renaissance Culture. In: Bracht Branham and Goulet-Gazé, editors. *The Cynics: The Cynic Movement in Antiquity and Its Legacy*. Berkeley: University of California Press, 1996. p. 324.

[52] I Corinthians 3:18 cited in: Luther. *To the Christian Nobility*. p. 260.

[53] Luther. *To the Christian Nobility*. p. 292.

[54] Luther. *To the Christian Nobility*. p. 336. Despite his wider remit, Luther does give the reform of the universities (and schools) some attention, fearing that without reform, without committing themselves to the task of turning out 'men who are experts in the Holy Scriptures, men who can become bishops and priests, and stand in the front line against heretics, the devil, and all the world', these unreformed universities will become 'wide gates to hell' (ibid. pp. 336-43.).

[55] Luther. *To the Christian Nobility*. p. 264.

[56] Luther. *To the Christian Nobility*. p. 265.

[57] II Peter 2:1-3 cited in: Luther. *To the Christian Nobility*. p. 267. p. 267.

[58] Luther. *To the Christian Nobility*.

[59] Brown, Norman O. *Life Against Death: The Psychoanalytical Meaning of History (Second Edition)*. Middletown, Connecticut: Wesleyan University Press, 1985. p. 214.

[60] Luther cited in: Brown. *Life Against Death*. p. 215.

[61] Brown. *Life Against Death*. p. 216.

[62] Brown. *Life Against Death*. p. 215.

[63] Luther. *To the Christian Nobility*. p. 268.

[64] Luther. *To the Christian Nobility*. p. 269.

[65] Luther. *To the Christian Nobility*. p. 290.

[66] Luther. *To the Christian Nobility*. p. 272.

[67] Luther. *To the Christian Nobility*. p. 274.

[68] Luther cited in: Brown. *Life Against Death*. p. 202.

[69] Brown. *Life Against Death*. p. 202.

[70] Nietzsche. *The Gay Science*. §347.

[71] Wrathall, Mark A. *Heidegger and Unconcealment: Truth, Language and History*. Cambridge: Cambridge University Press, 2011. p. 199.

[72] Nietzsche. *Daybreak*. §117.

[73] Foucault. *Security, Territory, Population*. p. 235.

[74] Horkheimer, Max. Reason Against Itself: Some Remarks on Enlightenment. In: Schmidt, editor. *What Is Enlightenment? Eighteenth-Century Answers and Twentieth Century Questions*. Berkeley: University of California Press, 1996 [1946]. p. 365.

[75] Horkheimer. *Reason Against Itself*. p. 365.

[76] Nietzsche. *The Gay Science*. §347.

[77] Luther cited in: Brown. *Life Against Death*. p. 226.

V. Mass Cynicism

[1] Nietzsche. *Human, All Too Human*. §51.

[2] Depaepe, Marc and Smeyers, Paul. Educationalization as an ongoing modernization process. *Educational Theory* 2008; 58(4). pp. 380-1.

[3] Depaepe and Smeyers. *Educationalization as an ongoing modernization process*. pp. 380-1.

[4] We find the Inquisitor included in his 'cabinet of cynics'. See: Sloterdijk. *Critique of Cynical Reason*. pp. 182-95.

[5] Dostoyevsky, Fyodor. *The Brothers Karamazov*. London: Penguin, 2003 [1880]. p. 325.

[6] Sloterdijk. *Critique of Cynical Reason*. p. 183.

[7] Sloterdijk. *Critique of Cynical Reason*. p. 183.

[8] Sloterdijk. *Critique of Cynical Reason.* p. 186.

[9] Sloterdijk. *Critique of Cynical Reason.* p. 192.

[10] Sloterdijk. *Critique of Cynical Reason.* p. 194.

[11] Sloterdijk. *Critique of Cynical Reason.* p. 8.

[12] Shea. *The Cynic Enlightenment.* p. 5.

[13] Shea (*The Cynic Enlightenment*) explores various attempts to revive Cynicism ranging from Diderot and D'Alembert, to Wieland, Rousseau and Sade.

[14] Shea. *The Cynic Enlightenment.* p. 132.

[15] Shea. *The Cynic Enlightenment..* p. ix.

[16] This is Stanley's gloss of Sloterdijk's argument regarding modern cynicism: Stanley, Sharon. Retreat from Politics: The Cynic in Modern Times. *Polity* 2007; 39(3). p. 385.

[17] Shea notes two early manifestations of this more strident cynicism: Diderot's depiction of *Rameau's Nephew* and various depictions by Sade, in particular the character Dolmancé in *Philosophy of the Boudoir.* Here connections with ancient Cynicism are still apparent, though only through a modern 'transvaluation' of key Cynic values, which is at the same time a destruction of key elements of the Cynic tradition (Shea. *The Cynic Enlightenment.* p. 110). Hence Rameau makes mischief by unmasking 'the pretenses and the corruption of the mid-eighteenth-century Parisian literati' but nevertheless accepts it as a "fait accompli" and 'accommodates himself to [that] reality as best he can' (ibid. p. 59). Absent here is the Cynic drive to overthrow the social order such hypocrisies reveal. Similarly, the Cynic's free and courageous speech becomes in Rameau mere impudence, a form of entertainment. The Cynic's appeal to a life lived according to nature (designed to cast light on the pretensions of civilized existence), is repeated in Rameau, but nature is now redefined as a battle for survival, recommending self-interested compliance with the corrupted norms of one's social habitat. The Cynic mantra 'deface the currency' is interpreted not to subvert the norms governing one's existence, but to attack the ideals foisted on one's existence by a small group of philosophers. Again, justified here, is Rameau's

attachment to the status quo (see: ibid. pp. 59-61). Rameau is not a cynic in the late modern sense, however. He, unlike his late modern descendants, still has the energy and appetite for combative, prolonged confrontations... Sade, by contrast, subverts Cynicism by transforming the 'frank Cynic' into the 'master of hypocrisy' (Dolmancé helps Eugéne to 'see through the veneer of our moral codes' whilst instructing her in deceit and subterfuge so that she may keep her infidelities hidden (ibid. p. 111). Extended to the public realm Sade's cynicism becomes a parody of its ancestor, where the Cynic injunction to live in accordance with nature (designed in part to free the Cynic from the moral force of shame and question what it means to be human) becomes a social norm that 'makes free sex an obligation, not an option' (ibid. p. 126). Again, the cynicism of Sade's characters is more strident (to say the least) than that with which we are accustomed. Though a taste for scandal remains, our late modern cynic is more prone to be publicly scandalized than privately scandalous, establishing a strange link between perverse enjoyment and moral indignation.

[18] Sloterdijk. *Critique of Cynical Reason*. p. 6.

[19] Stanley. *The Cynic in Modern Times*. p. 391.

[20] Žižek, Slavoj. *Trouble in Paradise: From the End of History to the End of Capitalism*. London: Penguin, 2015. pp. 67-9.

[21] Sloterdijk. *Critique of Cynical Reason*. p. xvi.

[22] Sloterdijk. *Critique of Cynical Reason*. p. xxxii.

[23] Sloterdijk. *Critique of Cynical Reason*. p. 6.

[24] Sloterdijk. *Critique of Cynical Reason*. p. 6.

[25] Sloterdijk. *Critique of Cynical Reason*. p. 5.

[26] As Freud claimed, melancholia is difficult to overcome, as it is impossible to fully reconcile oneself to a loss one can only vaguely comprehend (see: Freud, Sigmund. Mourning and Melancholia. In: Strachey, editor. *Volume XIV. The Standard Edition of the Complete Psychological Works of Sigmund Freud*. London: Vintage, 2001 [1917]).

[27] 'Not only does he [the melancholic] not detach himself from the object, but he internalizes it – consequently *preventing the*

possibility to detach' (Ferber, Ilit. Melancholy Philosophy: Freud and Benjamin. *E-rea* 2006; 4(1)).

[28] Strictly speaking these ideals were always inoperable anyway. What has changed, to be more precise, is that the promises that were attached to such ideals have become inoperable.

[29] For some exemplary media accounts by teachers leaving the profession see: Sloggett, Chris. This is why I am among the thousands leaving teaching this month: Excessive accountability, an unhealthy level of suspicion and an obsession with statistics has made this an impossible career path. *The Independent*. Thursday 10 July 2014. Burton, Sam. A teacher speaks out: 'I'm effectively being forced out of a career that I wanted to love'. *The Independent*. Monday 15 September 2014. Hawkins, Pauline. Why I'm Resigning After 11 Years as a Teacher. *Huffington Post*. 16 April 2014. And for accounts by academics leaving the profession see: Jarosinski, Eric. #failedintellectual. *The Chronicle of Higher Education*. 30 June 2014. Warner, Marina. Diary. *London Review of Books*. 11 September 2014. Katsari, Constantina. Leaving academia: 'I can offer more to the public outside the university system'. *The Guardian*. Friday 22 November 2013. See also the tragic case of Stefan Grimm: Parr, Chris. Imperial College professor Stefan Grimm 'was given grant income target'. *Times Higher Education*. 3 December 2014 2014.

[30] Allen, Ansgar. *Benign Violence: Education in and beyond the Age of Reason*. Basingstoke: Palgrave Macmillan, 2014.

[31] Gide, André. *Strait is the Gate*. London: Penguin, 1979 [1909]. p. 63.

[32] Bernstein, Basil. Education cannot compensate for society. *New Society* 1970; 387.

[33] A phrase I borrow from: Seneca. *Letters from a Stoic*. p. 36.

[34] Exemplary of this condition is the following appeal, attached to an email from the general secretary of the University College Union seeking to rally support for a strike ballot: "Dear colleague. If you agree with Steve, time is running out. The ballot closes next week and with a bank holiday coming up, you

really need to vote now. Please return your ballot. *"What I do as a teacher, tutor, lecturer and researcher generates value and will go on generating value. I am not only worth far more than I am or have ever been paid, I am worth far more than I ever will be paid. I have worked and studied hard over a long time to become and stay good at a difficult job and I deserve to be earning more, not less, as the years go by and as I keep learning from my experience in the profession. The same is true of the vast majority of people working in education as educators, and yet the idea of 'reward' is only respected for the so-called 'leaders' (colleagues with management responsibilities). Enough! Time for the union to do what unions are needed for: protect the pay and working conditions of its membership."* Do you agree? Vote TODAY.' (Email to UCU membership dated 28 April 2016).

[35] On 'improvement' see: Flint, Kevin and Peim, Nick. *Rethinking the Education Improvement Agenda: A Critical Philosophical Approach.* London: Continuum, 2012.

[36] Webb, Darren. Pedagogies of Hope. *Studies in Philosophy and Education* 2013; 32.

[37] Curwin, Richard. Cynicism is Contagious; So Is Hope. *www.edutopia.org* April 17, 2013.

[38] Ecclestone, Kathryn and Lewis, Lydia. Interventions for resilience in educational settings: challenging policy discourses of risk and vulnerability. *Journal of Education Policy* 2014; 29(2).

[39] Brown, Kate. Re-moralising 'vulnerability'. *People, Place & Policy* 2012; 6(1).

[40] Nietzsche, Friedrich. Twilight of the Idols or How to Philosophize with a Hammer. *Twilight of the Idols and The Anti-Christ.* London: Penguin, 2003 [1889].

[41] Ahmed, Sara. Multiculturalism and the Promise of Happiness. *New Formations* 2007-2008; 63(Winter).

[42] This new formation has been described by Sara Ahmed as 'the happiness turn' (Ahmed, Sara. Editorial. The Happiness Turn. *New Formations* 2007-2008; 63(Winter)).

[43] Love, Heather. Compulsory Happiness And Queer Existence. *New Formations* 2007-2008; 63(Winter).

[44] Ahmed, Sara. Affect Aliens: Happiness as a Cultural Politics. In: Satterthwaite, Piper and Sikes, editors. *Power in the Academy*. Stoke on Trent: Trentham Books, 2009.

[45] Levering, Bas, Ramaekers, Stefan and Smeyers, Paul. The Narrative of a Happy Childhood: on the presumption of parents' power and the demand for integrity. *Power and Education* 2009; 1(1).

[46] Ahmed. *Happiness as a Cultural Politics*.

[47] Colebrook, Claire. Narrative Happiness and the Meaning of Life. *New Formations* 2007-2008; 63(Winter).

[48] Kotchemidova, Christina. From Good Cheer to "Drive-by Smiling": A Social History of Cheerfulness. *Journal of Social History* 2005; 39(1).

[49] Horkheimer. *Reason Against Itself*. p. 366.

[50] Horkheimer. *Reason Against Itself*. pp. 366-7.

[51] Foucault, Michel. *The Birth of Biopolitics: Lectures at the Collège de France 1978-1979*. Basingstoke: Palgrave Macmillan, 2008 [1979].

[52] Sloterdijk. *Critique of Cynical Reason*. p. 7.

[53] Nietzsche. *The Will to Power*. p. 35.

[54] Nietzsche. *The Will to Power*. p. 32.

[55] Nietzsche. *The Will to Power*. p. 15.

VI. Insults and Obscenities

[1] Diogenes. *Diogenes the Cynic: Sayings and Anecdotes*. Oxford: Oxford University Press, 2012. p. 17.

[2] Sloterdijk. *Critique of Cynical Reason*. p. 168 (original emphasis).

[3] Laughter is not the only available technique. Parody, for example, was used by Diogenes to mock the authority of reason. Accordingly, Diogenes used the conventional

philosophical form of a syllogism to justify theft. The 'butt of the joke is its form', seeking to provide a 'jarring contrast between the formal protocols of reason and the paradoxically Cynic' conclusion it leads to (see Bracht Branham, R. Defacing the Currency: Diogenes' Rhetoric and the *Invention* of Cynicism. In: Bracht Branham and Goulet-Gazé, editors. *The Cynics: The Cynic Movement in Antiquity and Its Legacy*. Berkeley: University of California Press, 1996. p. 94.).

[4] Foucault. *The Courage of Truth*. p. 165.

[5] As Sloterdijk observes: 'Diogenes taught masturbation by practical example, as cultural progress, mind you, not as regression to the animalistic.' (Sloterdijk. *Critique of Cynical Reason*. p. 168.)

[6] Dio Chrysostom, Oration 8.

[7] Sloterdijk. *Critique of Cynical Reason*. p. 151.

[8] Cynic attitudes were passed on chiefly through an oral tradition. Some of the first Cynics do appear to have written, but almost all of their works have been lost. These works were, moreover, said to be rather unconventional, either parodying conventional forms of writing (such as the philosophical treatise), or subverting convention by adopting non-literary forms such as the diatribe (see: Bracht Branham. *Diogenes' Rhetoric and the Invention of Cynicism.*).

[9] Cutler, Ian. *Cynicism from Diogenes to Dilbert*. Jefferson, North Carolina: McFarland, 2005. p. 25.

[10] Bracht Branham and Goulet-Gazé. *The Cynics: Introduction*.

[11] Foucault. *The Courage of Truth*. p. 202.

[12] Foucault. *The Courage of Truth*. pp. 196-7.

[13] 'You have even managed to diminish the prestige of philosophy in general' (Julian. To the Cynic Heracleios (Oration 7). In: Dobbin, editor. *The Cynic Philosophers from Diogenes to Julian*. London: Penguin, 2012 [362]. p. 225.).

[14] Dobbin. *The Cynic Philosophers*. p. 210.

[15] Foucault. *The Courage of Truth*. p. 198.

[16] Krueger, Derek. The Bawdy and Society: The Shamelessness of Diogenes in Roman Imperial Culture. In: Bracht Branham and Goulet-Gazé, editors. *The Cynics: The Cynic Movement in Antiquity and Its Legacy*. Berkeley: University of California Press, 1996. p. 226.

[17] He had in mind those 'moving from city to city or camp to camp and insulting the rich and prominent in all such places while associating with society's dregs' (Julian. *To the Cynic Heracleios*. p. 223.).

[18] Julian. *Against the Ignorant Cynics*. p. 198.

[19] Cited in: Billerbeck, Margarethe. The Ideal Cynic from Epictetus to Julian. In: Bracht Branham and Goulet-Gazé, editors. *The Cynics: The Cynic Movement in Antiquity and Its Legacy*. Berkeley: University of California Press, 1996. p. 216. For a slightly different translation see: Julian. *To the Cynic Heracleios*. p. 226.

[20] Julian. *Against the Ignorant Cynics*. p. 196.

[21] Cited in: Billerbeck. *The Ideal Cynic*. p. 216.

[22] Such is the 'Neoplatonic coloring' of Julian's speech (Billerbeck. *The Ideal Cynic*. p. 216.).

[23] Julian. *To the Cynic Heracleios*. p. 226.

[24] Julian. *To the Cynic Heracleios*. p. 207.

[25] Bracht Branham and Goulet-Gazé. *The Cynics: Introduction*. pp. 21-3.

[26] Branham. *Diogenes' Rhetoric and the Invention of Cynicism*. p. 87.

[27] Laertius, Diogenes. *Lives of Eminent Philosophers II (Loeb Classical Library)*. Cambridge, Massachusetts: Harvard University Press, 1931 [3rd century CE]. 6.22-3.

[28] Bracht Branham. *Diogenes' Rhetoric and the Invention of Cynicism*. p. 89.

[29] The idea virtue can only be cultivated in a rarefied atmosphere is so common to Western philosophy and its educational legacies it is almost futile to dignify it with a single footnote. Effectively, it is believed that 'virtue only comes to a

character which has been thoroughly schooled and trained and brought to a pitch of perfection by unremitting practice' (Seneca. *Letters from a Stoic*. pp. 176-7.). It is the possession of 'wise men'. Indeed the exclusivity of virtue, achieved through wisdom, is 'the best thing about her'. There is 'about wisdom [and the virtue it cultivates] a nobility and magnificence in the fact that she...is not a blessing given to all and sundry' (ibid. p. 162.).

[30] Foucault. *The Courage of Truth*. p. 167.

[31] Diogenes. *Sayings and Anecdotes*. pp. 10-11.

[32] Foucault. *The Courage of Truth*. p. 258.

[33] Foucault. *The Courage of Truth*. p. 194.

[34] Plato. *Phaedo*. 66b-c.

[35] Foucault. *The Courage of Truth*. p. 171.

[36] Foucault. *The Courage of Truth*. p. 222.

[37] Foucault. *The Courage of Truth*. pp. 221-5.

[38] Diogenes. *Sayings and Anecdotes*. p. 25.

[39] As Foucault argues, we can see traces of this 'Cynic game of humiliation' in Christian humility: 'From Cynic humiliation to Christian humility there is an entire history of the humble, of disgrace, shame, and scandal through shame, which is very important historically and, once again, quite foreign to the standard morality of the Greeks and Romans'. Foucault argues nevertheless, that 'we should distinguish the future Christian humility, which is a state, a mental attitude manifesting itself and testing itself in the humiliations one suffers, from this Cynic dishonor, which is a game with conventions of honor and dishonor in which the Cynic, at the very point when he plays the most disgraceful role, brings out his pride and supremacy. Cynic pride relies on these tests. The Cynic asserts his sovereignty, his mastery through these tests of humiliation, whereas Christian humiliation, or rather, humility, is a renunciation of oneself.' (Foucault. *The Courage of Truth*. p. 262.)

[40] Foucault. *The Courage of Truth*. p. 272.

[41] Foucault. *The Courage of Truth*. p. 278.

[42] Diogenes. *Sayings and Anecdotes*. p. 24.

[43] Foucault. *The Courage of Truth.* p. 279.

[44] Foucault. *The Courage of Truth.* p. 279.

[45] Foucault. *The Courage of Truth.* p. 280.

[46] Foucault. *The Courage of Truth.* p. 280.

[47] Foucault. *The Courage of Truth.* p. 280.

[48] Shea. *The Cynic Enlightenment.* p. 10.

[49] Shea. *The Cynic Enlightenment.* p. 9.

[50] Foucault. *The Courage of Truth.* p. 227.

[51] Foucault. *The Courage of Truth.* p. 244.

[52] Foucault. *The Courage of Truth.* p. 244.

[53] Foucault. *The Courage of Truth.* p. 253.

[54] Foucault. *The Courage of Truth.* p. 253.

[55] Bracht Branham. *Diogenes' Rhetoric and the Invention of Cynicism.* p. 86.

[56] Foucault. *The Courage of Truth.* p. 208.

[57] Foucault claims this attempt to reactualize the original core of a philosophy was essential to Platonism and Aristotelianism, and was also present in Stoicism and Epicureanism, though in the latter attempts were also made to reactualize a form of existence. With Cynicism, the importance of reactualizing a form of existence almost completely replaces the drive to define oneself in relation to the essential doctrinal core of the tradition (see: Foucault. *The Courage of Truth.* p. 209.). Of course, attempts to reactualize the original core of Cynicism were indeed made, but these efforts were made by those seeking to integrate aspects of Cynicism into other philosophical traditions. Consequently, it was necessary to idealize Diogenes in particular, and 'purge his portrait of any features that might shock or keep off potential followers' (see: Billerbeck. *The Ideal Cynic.* p. 205.).

[58] Foucault. *The Courage of Truth.* p. 209.

[59] Foucault. *The Courage of Truth.* p. 209.

[60] This pursuit of animality was a tactic used to disrupt cultural conventions the status of which depended upon their elevation

above base inclinations. By resorting to animality, and giving it a certain priority over more refined 'human' traits, the Cynic was not expressing a belief in nature. A normative conception of nature did not provide a foundation for Cynic philosophy. Interpretations vary, of course, but those suspicious of the common view that nature was Cynicism's foundational belief, claim that on a closer look at the anecdotes collected by Diogenes Laertius that 'purport to quote Diogenes [of Sinope] verbatim, nowhere does he show any interest in nature as a philosophical concept' (Bracht Branham. *Diogenes' Rhetoric and the Invention of Cynicism*. p. 96.)

[61] Foucault. *The Courage of Truth*. p. 181.

[62] Foucault. *The Courage of Truth*. p. 183.

[63] Foucault. *The Courage of Truth*. p. 182.

[64] Foucault. *The Courage of Truth*. p. 183.

[65] Foucault. *The Courage of Truth*. p. 320.

[66] Foucault. *The Courage of Truth*. p. 190.

[67] Nietzsche. *Beyond Good and Evil*. § 269 (my emphasis).

[68] Adlam and Scanlon. *Personality Disorder and Homelessness: Membership and 'Unhoused Minds' in Forensic Settings*. p. 453.

[69] Sloterdijk. *Critique of Cynical Reason*. p. 194.

[70] Sloterdijk. *Critique of Cynical Reason*. p. 194.

[71] Boltanski, Luc and Chiapello, Eve. *The New Spirit of Capitalism*. London: Verso, 2007 [1999]. Boltanski, Luc. The Left after May 1968 and the longing for total revolution. *Thesis Eleven* 2002; 69.

[72] Cederström, Carl and Fleming, Peter. *Dead Man Working*. Winchester: Zero Books, 2011.

[73] This obsession with authenticity is reflected in the tendency for contestants of the UK *Big Brother* television game show to be the most authentic housemate. Contestants are perfectly aware of this; they frequently discuss the idea of having a 'game plan' to win, suspecting each other for having one and hence for being inauthentic. Of course, many declare that the ultimate game plan is to 'just be yourself'.

[74] Gardiner, Michael E. The Grandchildren of Marx and Coca-Cola: Lefebvre, Utopia and the 'Recuperation' of Everyday Life. In: Hayden and El-Ojeili, editors. *Globalization and Utopia: Critical Essays*. Basingstoke: Palgrave Macmillan, 2009. p. 228.

[75] Laertius. *Lives of Eminent Philosophers II*. 6.76-7.

[76] The absurd (to which I return in *Chapter IX*) is given content by Albert Camus in *The Myth of Sisyphus*, a book in which Camus takes pains to explain that once the absurd becomes apparent the only 'truly philosophical problem' is whether or not to commit suicide (Camus, Albert. *The Myth of Sisyphus*. London: Penguin, 2000 [1942]. p. 5). In educational settings however, the absurd remains largely hidden from view, or at least, is only superficially felt despite longstanding disparity between our highest educational ideals and the unremittingly grubby nature of educational realities that remain subservient to relations of power, class and capital. This disparity perfectly exemplifies what Camus might describe as the presence of the absurd in education (where the hopes themselves, or the unremitting nature of reality are not absurd; the absurd is generated in the impossible relationship established between them; see ibid. p. 24). The presence of the absurd in education is not generally recognised, since by profession, educators are reflexively buffered from perceiving it, blinkered into believing that despite it all education can be 'redeemed' (The idea that education can be redeemed persists against all the evidence. This point is made by Nick Peim, who attacks the 'powerful mythology of redemption' which dominates educational thought and practice See: Peim, Nick. The Big Other: An Offer You Can't Refuse - or Accept, in Some Cases. Education as Onto-Theological Principle (Empire): An Anti-Manifesto. *Other Education: The Journal of Educational Alternatives* 2012; 1(1)). Since the absurd is beyond the educator's grasp, the challenge becomes one of establishing a new, inverted relationship between the absurd and suicide, approaching suicide in order to discover the absurd. And having sought suicide so as to experience the absurd, 'the real effort' for those remaining in the profession 'is to stay there' within that experience, continuing to work in an educational landscape that has come to appear

devastatingly odd, refusing the temptation to fall back on the old reassurances that education must, somehow, somewhere, have a core worth rescuing (Camus. *The Myth of Sisyphus*. p. 10). The challenge begins as one encounters the absurd, since it is so tempting to recoil, retreating from this disconcerting encounter either into the consolations of hope and belief, or through despair to that ultimate exit, which is suicide. Living with the absurd requires that one endure and affirm an impossible tension never to be resolved, between 'the mind that desires and the world that disappoints', between our 'nostalgia for unity' and meaning, and this intransigent, 'fragmented universe' (ibid. p. 37). Hence Camus attacks suicide as an expression of weakness. It represents an escape route for those who cannot stand the absurd, those who will not be consoled and cannot live without consolation. With this in mind, Camus portrays suicide as a form of capitulation to more dominant forces. Suicide constitutes for him a species of acceptance of those very forces 'at its extreme' (ibid. p. 41). Presumably this act of final submission could be to forces ranging from the more grandiose but immediately felt exertions of an indifferent universe, to those more straightforward forces which make suicide practically possible, such as the force of gravity or chemical reaction. To return to our problem then. If Camus was correct to characterise suicide in this way, it would appear that to approach the absurd through suicide ignores his basic insight, which insists that suicide is a form of surrender. For this tactic to make sense – whereby the absurd is approached by first risking oneself – we must seek out a form of exit which does not seek escape from an absurd existence it can no longer bear. It would desire instead to transform that existence, and render it more palpably absurd, if only by the force of example. Here we must hold in view a type of suicide of the kind Diogenes attempted; an impossible suicide in other words, since it refused all assistance, declining to give in to or take advantage of dominant forces, affirming its decision without capitulation.

[77] Cynicism has nevertheless been interpreted as 'an act of individual self-assertion', and reduced thereby to a species of individualism. However, as Shea observes (building on Foucault), this fails to notice a basic connection between the

Cynic act and the truth it manifests, where Cynicism seeks to 'redefine the relation between the self and truth' and thereby redefine the relationship between subject and power, by bearing witness to other possible forms of embodied truth (Shea. *The Cynic Enlightenment.* p. 176). In short, the Cynic is labouring to disturb a broader framework. This mode of resistance becomes only more significant in an age where, according to Foucault, we are increasingly constituted as self-constituting agents of power. In order to contest power it is necessary to contest how it is manifested in those subjects of power who are now, increasingly, its agents.

[78] Freire, Paulo. *Pedagogy in Process: The Letters to Guinea-Bissau.* London: Writers and Readers Publishing Cooperative, 1978. pp. 103-4.

[79] See: Cabral, Amilcar. The Weapon of Theory. *Unity and Struggle: Speeches and Writings of Amilcar Cabral.* New York: Monthly Review Press, 1979 [1966]. p. 136. Crucially, Cabral also insisted that 're-Africanization' would be necessary in the death and rebirth of Guinea-Bissau intellectuals (see: Cabral, Amilcar. National Liberation and Culture. *Unity and Struggle: Speeches and Writings of Amilcar Cabral.* New York: Monthly Review Press, 1979 [1070]. p. 145). The suggestion that the 'revolutionary petty bourgeoisie must be capable of committing *suicide* as a class' (Cabral. *The Weapon of Theory.* p. 136), was based on Cabral's observation that the petty bourgeois class was in such a precarious position (in contemporary Cape Verde and Guinea) that class suicide was a viable alternative to siding with the Portuguese colonialists.

[80] Freire. *Pedagogy in Process.* p. 103.

[81] Freire. *Pedagogy in Process.* p. 104.

[82] Freire's invitation to commit 'class suicide' (or as Jonathan Kozol put it in his Forward to the book: that those 'who have grown up, lived and studied, in a privileged situation, must 'die as a class' and be 'reborn in consciousness', Freire, *Pedagogy in Process.* p. 3.) is rarely mentioned. For an exception see: Mayo, Peter. Synthesizing Gramsci and Freire: possibility for a

theory of radical adult education. *International Journal of Lifelong Education* 1994; 13(2).

[83] Foucault, Michel. Interview with Michel Foucault. In: Faubion, editor. *Essential Works of Foucault 1954-1984. Volume 3*. London: Penguin, 2002 [1978]. p. 241.

[84] Vonnegut. *Playboy Interview*. p. 214.

VII. Spirit of Heaviness

[1] Foucault. *Security, Territory, Population*. p. 183.

[2] Foucault. *Security, Territory, Population*. p. 182.

[3] See: Foucault. *On the Government of the Living*. p. 291.

[4] Foucault. *On the Government of the Living*. pp. 207-8.

[5] Hunter. *Rethinking the school*. p. xxi.

[6] Blanchot, Maurice. *Lautréamont and Sade*. Stanford: Stanford University Press, 2004 [1949]. p. 39.

[7] Lingis, Alphonso. Translator's Introduction. *Sade My Neighbour*. Evanston, Illinois: Northwestern University Press, 1991. p. x.

[8] The educational intent of Sade's work is not only modeled internally. *Juliette*, according to one footnote, is intended for lady readers: 'Hot-blooded and lewdly disposed ladies, these are words to the wise, hark attentively to them: they are addressed not only to Juliette but to yourselves also; if your intelligence is in any sense comparable to hers, you'll not fail to extract great benefit from them' (Sade, Marquis de. *Juliette*. New York: Grove Press, 1968 [1797]. p. 340).

[9] Though it is a woman, Juliette, who is the libertine hero of the book of the same name, and though the book is addressed to lady readers, our hero rarely encounters her match in libertine women, and finds she has much to teach most of the women she meets. So, for example, to Princess Borghese she remarks: 'Among libertine women I have never encountered your superior... But there are...scores and scores of little habits, dirty and furtive ones, loathsome and ugly ones, crapulous and brutal ones, which, perhaps, my gentle dove, you are still to make

acquaintance of' (Sade. *Juliette*. p. 709). For lessons in mastery, with the exception perhaps of the sorceress Durand, Juliette looks most often, and more beseechingly to men.

[10] Sade. *Juliette*. p. 181.

[11] The moment he detects her falter and recoil before his imagined crimes Saint-Fond, Juliette's greatest sponsor, abandons her and has her quit Paris (and later France) leaving behind all she has acquired through his largesse and protection. This is after so much success, after Juliette has given him so much cause to admire her grotesque affinity for libertinage. But for her moment of weakness, Juliette had otherwise reached that exalted and most libertine state of 'numbed indifference'. It is at this point, once so much has been achieved in crime and horror, Juliette recalls, 'that virtue makes a final effort inside us... this is the moment, beware of it, when long-forgotten prejudices reappear' (Sade. *Juliette*. pp. 548-9.). Eventually Juliette rises to power once again, whilst Saint-Fond falls foul of her accomplice, Noirceuil.

[12] Sade. *Juliette*. p. 285. Juliette is frequently upbraided by her teachers, but is on the lookout too for inconsistencies and weaknesses in those who instruct her. She questions Saint-Fond's mastery on more than one occasion; for allowing himself to be in debt to others (ibid. p. 245), and for allowing himself to believe in some form of afterlife (ibid. p. 370). Meanwhile, she accuses Clairwil (who will eventually die by her hand) of a weakened atheism (ibid. p. 451).

[13] Sade. *Juliette*. p. 263.

[14] There is little patience for teaching those who do not swiftly acquire libertine mastery. The libertine educator, like the libertine Pope, is under an obligation 'to make fools of the simple' (Sade. *Juliette*. p. 757). Fellow libertines wanton enough to deserve some respect, such as the Countess Donis (who, Juliette narrates 'was already almost a match for me in wickedness') do, however, still manage to incite Juliette to teach (ibid. p. 634). This is because Juliette finds in those of similar cast an opportunity for libertinage. In Donis she swiftly acquires a wealthy accomplice. If she also teaches Donis for a short

interval, it is only so as to acquire a better partner in crime, and perhaps hone her own philosophy too, as she holds forth before a willing listener. But Donis is soon sacrificed, having betrayed herself as still imperfectly libertine. Juliette has little patience for teaching. As she explains to her student and unwitting victim, any residual virtue 'fairly turns my stomach' (ibid. p. 646). Another student, Duchess Grillo, is tolerated for longer since she is at first a great source of pleasure. But as soon as she proves unresponsive to her teachings Juliette loses patience: 'that was the moment I took the resolve to destroy her' (ibid. p. 722). Princess Borghese is also finally despatched, after many libertine adventures by Juliette's side. She is cast into a volcano because, in the end, she 'lacked depth and rigor in her principles; timorous, still in prejudice's grip, apt at any moment to give way before a reverse, and who, owing to nothing more than this one weakness, was unsuitable company' for a woman as corrupt as Juliette (ibid. p. 1019).

[15] This is unusual in the prolix context of Sade's writing.

[16] Sade. *Juliette*. p. 485.

[17] Sade. *Juliette*. p. 159.

[18] Gallop, Jane. The Immoral Teachers. *Yale French Studies* 1982; 63. p. 118.

[19] Gallop. *The Immoral Teachers*. p. 126.

[20] Kings are ridiculed accordingly: 'In our day there is nothing more superfluous than a king.' Having become weak, their authority rests on 'nothing solider than opinion', which is fickle and will most assuredly betray them. These kings, seated at one remove and in luxury neglect, moreover, the 'first virtue demanded of anyone who wishes to be a ruler of men' which is 'knowledge of them'. Tucked away, 'perpetually stunned and fuddled by their flatteries', monarchs are not able to 'sift nor scan' those they rule (Sade. *Juliette*. p. 568). To master men one must live among them and examine them most intimately.

[21] Gallop. *The Immoral Teachers*. p. 122.

[22] Hence 'the most enjoyable crimes are the motiveless ones. The victim must be perfectly innocent: if we have sustained

some harm from him it legitimates the harm we do him' (Sade. *Juliette*. p. 702).

[23] It suits my exposition to treat Man, God, and finally Nature in that sequence. But it must be remembered that Sade works away at each problem (the problems posed by Man, God and Nature) throughout his texts and in no particular order. This is, as Jane Gallop argues, no simple dialectical arrangement (see: Gallop, Jane. *Intersections: A reading of Sade with Bataille, Blanchot, and Klossowski*. Lincoln: University of Nebraska Press, 1981). Sade's attacks are too frenzied for that.

[24] Blanchot. *Lautréamont and Sade*. p. 7.

[25] With regard to reason, Sade confronts the idea that a better use of reason, and better knowledge of and more thoroughgoing attempt to master our material existence 'will make possible a better individual and social morality' (Klossowski, Pierre. *Sade My Neighbour*. Evanston, Illinois: Northwestern University Press, 1991 [1967/1947]. p. 81). As Pierre Klossowski argued, Sade foresees instead from reason 'not the arrival of a happier era for humanity, but only the beginning of tragedy', which Sade not only consciously and deliberately accepts, but also realises in his writing, making use of reason to monstrous effect (ibid.).

[26] Sade. *Juliette*. p. 415.

[27] Sade. *Juliette*. p. 14.

[28] Blanchot. *Lautréamont and Sade*. p. 20.

[29] As the libertine Princess Borghese declares: 'The stocks, the pillory, the scaffold itself would for me be a privilege, the throne of delight, upon it I'd cry death defiance, and discharge in the pleasure of perishing the victim of my crimes and over the idea that in future my name would a byword for evil, at whose mere mention generations of men would tremble... I see the abyss yawning at my feet, and jubilantly I hurl myself over the brink' (Sade. *Juliette*. pp. 663-4). Elsewhere Juliette says something similar: 'There is nothing I fear less in the world than the noose... If ever a judge sends me to the scaffold, you will see me go forward with light and impudent step' (ibid. p. 1014).

[30] Blanchot. *Lautréamont and Sade*. p. 21.

[31] Blanchot. *Lautréamont and Sade*. p. 24.

[32] See: Sade, Marquis de. *The 120 Days of Sodom and other writings*. New York: Grove Press, 1966 [1785]. p. 362. And not only comparison is suspect, pleasure itself is problematic. The libertine should, in principle, be able perpetrate the worst crimes with the coolest temperament, without being fired up and into action by the atrocities occasioned: 'Crime is the torch that should fire the passions.' Whereas the opposite ('passion firing her to crime') is infinitely suspect. We are told that 'the difference is enormous', where the latter signifies, for the libertine concerned, that she is still plagued by a 'ruinous sensibility' (Sade. *Juliette*. p. 475).

[33] Klossowski. *Sade My Neighbour*. p. 79.

[34] Blanchot. *Lautréamont and Sade*. pp. 18-9.

[35] Blanchot. *Lautréamont and Sade*. p. 25.

[36] Cavarero. *In Spite of Plato*. p. 55.

[37] Blanchot. *Lautréamont and Sade*. p. 25.

[38] Blanchot. *Lautréamont and Sade*. p. 26.

[39] Though Simone de Beauvoir's account is divergent in so many other respects, here there is agreement (see: Beauvoir, Simone de. Must We Burn Sade? In: Wainhouse and Seaver, editors. *The 120 Days of Sodom and other writings - Marquis de Sade*. New York: Grove Press, 1966 [1951]. p. 21).

[40] Beauvoir. *Must We Burn Sade?* p. 29. This elision between the philosopher and the libertine is not exaggerated. In Sade's writing accomplished philosophy and perfect libertinage are virtually synonymous, where the most horrific crimes are only achieved through the most perfect philosophy.

[41] Nietzsche. *Twilight of the Idols*. p. 46.

[42] Nietzsche. *The Gay Science*. §125.

[43] Blanchot. *Lautréamont and Sade*. p. 28.

[44] Sade. *Juliette*. p. 20.

[45] Blanchot. *Lautréamont and Sade*. p. 28.

[46] Sade. *Juliette*. p. 967.

[47] Blanchot. *Lautréamont and Sade*. p. 29.

[48] Blanchot. *Lautréamont and Sade*. p. 31.

[49] Blanchot. *Lautréamont and Sade*. p. 29.

[50] Blanchot. *Lautréamont and Sade*. p. 31.

[51] Blanchot. *Lautréamont and Sade*. p. 32.

[52] Sade. *Juliette*. p. 782.

[53] Blanchot. *Lautréamont and Sade*. p. 32.

[54] Sade. *Juliette*. p. 611.

[55] Blanchot. *Lautréamont and Sade*. p. 35.

[56] Blanchot. *Lautréamont and Sade*. p. 35.

[57] Klossowski. *Sade My Neighbour*. p. 92.

[58] Klossowski. *Sade My Neighbour*. p. 97.

[59] Klossowski. *Sade My Neighbour*. p. 97.

[60] Horkheimer, Max and Adorno, Theodor. *Dialectic of Enlightenment: Philosophical Fragments*. Stanford: Stanford University Press, 2002 [1947]. p. 69.

[61] Klossowski. *Sade My Neighbour*. p. 96.

[62] Horkheimer and Adorno. *Dialectic of Enlightenment*. p. 69.

[63] Horkheimer and Adorno. *Dialectic of Enlightenment*. p. 65.

[64] Sade. *Juliette*. p. 730.

[65] Nietzsche. *The Will to Power*.

[66] See: Straehler-Pohl, Hauke and Pais, Alexandre. Learning to fail and learning from failure - ideology at work in a mathematics classroom. *Pedagogy, Culture & Society* 2014; 22(1). One educational response to failure is to argue that we should 'make failure an option', making it permissible for those who do not fit to opt out of the normative order of an educational system they cannot bear. Such non-normative others would be encouraged to follow other pathways to success (see: Steigler, Sam and Sullivan, Rachael E. How to 'fail' in school without really trying: queering pathways to success. *Pedagogy, Culture & Society* 2015; 23(1)). The problem with this kind of critique, I suspect, is that it would seem to perpetuate a belief in educational mastery by seeking to bleed out the effects of failure and diversify what it

means to succeed. This admittedly generous, and typically progressive response to the presence of failure in education is problematic, in that it defers the problem of failure, and hence, despite itself, leaves education essentially intact.

[67] Straehler-Pohl and Pais. *Learning to fail and learning from failure*. p. 81.

[68] Nietzsche, Friedrich. *Thus Spoke Zarathustra: A Book for Everyone and Nobody*. Oxford: Oxford University Press, 2005 [1883]. p. 36.

VIII. A Modern Fetish

[1] Ariès, Philippe. *The Hour of Our Death*. New York: Vintage, 2008 [1977]. p. 355.

[2] Ariès. *The Hour of Our Death*. p. 357.

[3] Ariès. *The Hour of Our Death*. pp. 357-8.

[4] Foucault, Michel. *Discipline and Punish: The Birth of The Prison*. London: Penguin, 1975 [1991].

[5] We find women carved swooning in stone relief upon their tombs. Upon these carvings death seemingly 'pierces like the arrow of an angel', the 'little death of sexual pleasure' associated with 'the final death of the body' (Ariès. *The Hour of Our Death*. p. 373).

[6] It is tempting to invoke some kind of zombie metaphor here. That metaphor has become strangely popular and informs the following collection of essays: Whelan, Andrew, Walker, Ruth and Moore, Christopher. *Zombies in the Academy: Living Death in Higher Education*. Bristol: Intellect, 2013. It is striking that even with this metaphor employed we are unlikely to fully confront our condition. This can be felt as one observes a zombie film. Do we not have a tendency still, to identify with the survivors rather than the zombie horde?

[7] This is reflected, Ben Jeffery argues, in the work of Michel Houellebecq. See: Jeffery, Ben. *Anti-Matter: Michel Houellebecq and Depressive Realism*. Winchester: Zero Books, 2011.

Notes

[8] Marx. *Capital I*. p. 170.

[9] Marx. *Capital I*. p. 179.

[10] Here Marx cites Goethe, claiming that 'our commodity owners think like Faust: 'In the beginning was the deed" (Marx. *Capital I*. p. 180.).

[11] Marx. *Capital I*. p. 187.

[12] Goddard, Roy and Payne, Mark. Criticality and the practice-based MA. *Journal of Education for Teaching* 2013; 39(1). p. 133.

[13] Goddard and Payne. Criticality and the practice-based MA. p. 133

[14] Shea. *The Cynic Enlightenment*. p. 199.

[15] Shea. *The Cynic Enlightenment*. p. 181.

[16] Shea. *The Cynic Enlightenment*. p. 181.

[17] Shea. *The Cynic Enlightenment*. p. 187.

[18] Foucault. *Interview with Michel Foucault*. p. 247.

[19] Foucault. *Interview with Michel Foucault*. p. 245.

[20] Rabinow, Paul. Foucault's Untimely Struggle. In: Falzon, O'Leary and Sawicki, editors. *A Companion to Foucault*. Chichester: Wiley-Blackwell, 2013. p. 192.

[21] Rabinow. Foucault's Untimely Struggle. p. 191.

[22] Rabinow. Foucault's Untimely Struggle. p. 192.

[23] Nietzsche. *Beyond Good and Evil*. § 206.

[24] Nietzsche. *Beyond Good and Evil*. § 205.

[25] Foucault spends some time explaining what he means by the phrase 'regime of truth' in: Foucault. *On the Government of the Living*. pp. 93-100. Foucault contests the idea that truths are self-evident, and that once they are admitted, the obligation to follow them is more or less automatic. Believing that this obligation is always a historical-cultural artefact, Foucault investigates how different regimes of truth have variously been tied to systems of obligation. His objective is to investigate how expressions of truth variously serve to constrain and bind all those involved in a particular regime of truth.

[26] Foucault. *The Courage of Truth*. p. 8.

[27] Foucault. *The Courage of Truth*. p. 11.

[28] Foucault. *The Courage of Truth*. pp. 12-3.

[29] Foucault. *The Courage of Truth*. p. 13.

[30] Foucault. *The Courage of Truth*. p. 25.

[31] Foucault. *The Courage of Truth*. p. 15.

[32] Foucault. *The Courage of Truth*. p. 16.

[33] Foucault. *The Courage of Truth*. p. 19.

[34] Foucault. *The Courage of Truth*. p. 24.

[35] Foucault. *The Courage of Truth*. pp. 28-9.

[36] Marx. *Capital I*. p. 270.

[37] Lawlor, Clark. *Consumption and Literature: The Making of the Romantic Disease*. Basingstoke: Palgrave Macmillan, 2006. p. 10.

[38] Dumas cited in: Lawlor. *Consumption and Literature*. p. 113.

[39] Lawlor. *Consumption and Literature*. p. 112.

[40] Lawlor. *Consumption and Literature*. p. 113.

[41] Sontag, Susan. Illness as Metaphor. *Illness as Metaphor and AIDS and Its Metaphors*. London: Penguin, 1978 [2002]. pp. 19-20.

[42] Nietzsche. *The Anti-Christ*. §53.

IX. The Absurd

[1] Laertius. *Lives of Eminent Philosophers II*. 6.31-2.

[2] Excerpt from a letter written by Nietzsche's sister to Clara Gelzer in 1882. Cited in: Salomé, Lou. *Nietzsche*. Urbana: University of Illinois Press, 2001 [1894]. p. li.

[3] Nietzsche, Friedrich. Attempt at Self-Criticism. *The Birth of Tragedy*. London: Penguin, 2003 [1886]. §1-2. The book is impossible, James Porter argues, since Nietzsche demonstrates in his writing the extreme, perhaps intractable difficulties faced as we seek to escape our metaphysical inheritance (Porter,

James. *The Invention of Dionysus: An Essay on The Birth of Tragedy*: Stanford University Press, 2000).

[4] A note of caution: Nietzsche typically invokes historical characters as vague cyphers, or code words, for broader structures of feeling. Consequently, as Michael Tanner argues in his Introduction to *The Birth of Tragedy,* the historical accuracy of these figures in Nietzsche's work 'may be at an ultimate discount' (Nietzsche. *The Birth of Tragedy.* p. xxi)

[5] The influence of which, Nietzsche claims, 'spread across posterity like a shadow lengthening in the evening sun' (Nietzsche. *The Birth of Tragedy.* §15).

[6] Nietzsche. *The Birth of Tragedy.* §9. Here Nietzsche is referring to Apolline qualities that exist in tension with the Dionysian aspect of Greek tragedy. This latter Dionysian aspect gives the lie to those boundaries established by Apolline art. Later these bounded qualities are transformed to become what Nietzsche refers to as the Socratic tendency, where self-knowledge and contemplation are now promoted in earnest. From this point on, so the argument goes, we become lost in an illusory world of bounded, knowledge-seeking individuals. As such, we are no longer disposed to confront the tragedy of human existence.

[7] Nietzsche. *The Birth of Tragedy.* §18.

[8] Camus, Albert. *The Fall.* London: Penguin, 1980 [1956]. p. 27.

[9] Nietzsche. *The Birth of Tragedy.* § 7.

[10] Nietzsche. *The Birth of Tragedy.* §18 (my emphasis).

[11] Nietzsche. *The Birth of Tragedy.* §3.

[12] Claiming that 'the worst thing of all for them would be to die soon, the second worst to die at all' (Nietzsche. *The Birth of Tragedy.* §3).

[13] Nietzsche. *The Birth of Tragedy.* §3.

[14] Nietzsche. *The Birth of Tragedy.* §3.

[15] Nietzsche. *The Birth of Tragedy.* §4.

[16] Nietzsche. *The Birth of Tragedy.* §4.

[17] Porter. *The Invention of Dionysus.* p. 86.

[18] Porter. *The Invention of Dionysus*. p. 85.

[19] Bernhard, Thomas. *Walking*. Chicago: University of Chicago Press. p. 7.

[20] Nietzsche. *The Birth of Tragedy*. §7.

[21] Nietzsche. *The Birth of Tragedy*. §7.

[22] Nietzsche. *The Birth of Tragedy*. §7.

[23] Nietzsche. *The Birth of Tragedy*. §18.

[24] Nietzsche. *The Birth of Tragedy*. §7.

[25] Nietzsche. *The Birth of Tragedy*. §7.

[26] Porter. *The Invention of Dionysus*. p. 113. This being Porter's translation from: Nietzsche. *The Birth of Tragedy*. §7.

[27] Nietzsche. *Human, All Too Human*. Preface §5.

[28] Nietzsche. *The Birth of Tragedy*. Attempt at Self-Criticism §1.

[29] Zaretsky, Robert. *A Life Worth Living*: Belknap Press, 2013. p. 32.

[30] Camus. *The Myth of Sisyphus*. p. ix.

[31] Here Camus held to the view that 'even within the limits of nihilism it is possible to find the means to proceed beyond nihilism' (Camus. *The Myth of Sisyphus*. p. ix).

[32] Camus, Albert. *The Outsider*. Harmondsworth: Penguin, 1972 [1942].

[33] 'It is not in his prereflective "indifference" or "honesty," but in his reflections before death, that Meursault becomes a semblance of the "absurd hero"' (Solomon, Robert. *Dark Feelings, Grim Thoughts: Experience and Reflection in Camus and Sartre*. Oxford: Oxford University Press, 2006. p. 26).

[34] Camus. *The Outsider*. p. 100.

[35] As argued, 'Meursault perversely [and eventually] sees that, on reflection, it can be seen that reflection is worthless' (Solomon. *Dark Feelings, Grim Thoughts*. p. 31). 'It is in the impassioned hopelessness of reflection, just before his execution, that Meursault faces 'the absurd' as a final revelation' and lays his heart open to the 'benign indifference of the universe' (ibid. p. 32).

[36] Camus. *The Outsider*. p. 120.

[37] It is conceivable that the absurd lost traction in stages: As Zaretsky observes, to the extent that post-war critics of *The Myth of Sisyphus* also felt the absurdity Camus described, they decided the best response was to adopt a position of ironic detachment. This was now the response of those who similarly felt the cosmic indifference to our situation. Yet by contrast to the inescapable pain the presence of absurdity once entailed for Camus, this more distant, ironic and philosophical response to the presence of absurdity seems to have come 'more easily to those who have lived mostly in the aftermath of World War II [rather] than those who lived through it' (Zaretsky. *A Life Worth Living*. pp. 49-50). So we have a sequence, where the coupling between absurdity and pain is replaced by a more detached coupling between absurdity and irony. Sticking with the idea of a staged departure, one might then suggest that today the position has advanced one stage further. We late moderns have been left only with the detached irony that the presence of the absurd once inspired. The absurd itself rarely appears to us now.

[38] Camus. *The Myth of Sisyphus*. p. 3.

[39] Zaretsky offers two contemporary examples: Firstly, 'the disparity between France's strength [in 1940]' and 'the suddenness of its collapse', and secondly, the disparity experienced by those millions of refugees fleeing from Belgium and northern France who, 'just days before they were pulled into the vortex created by the capsizing of the French republic, still believed stupidly in the permanence of their civil, legal, and political institutions, as well as the durability of their everyday lives' (Zaretsky. *A Life Worth Living*. p. 29). These lives were suddenly punctured in moments that could be 'as banal as an overheard conversation or a glimpsed interaction, or as extraordinary as a Stuka bearing down on you' (ibid. p. 30). Try though one might to return to normal, those who had experienced such absurdity would always remain, as Camus put it, at least 'just slightly out of tune' (ibid.).

[40] Camus. *The Myth of Sisyphus*. p. 15.

[41] Camus. *The Myth of Sisyphus*. p. 15

[42] Camus. *The Myth of Sisyphus*. p. 17.

[43] Camus. *The Myth of Sisyphus*. p. 22.

[44] Camus. *The Myth of Sisyphus*. p. 37.

[45] Camus. *The Myth of Sisyphus*. p. 17.

[46] Camus. *The Myth of Sisyphus*. pp. 17-8.

[47] Camus. *The Myth of Sisyphus*. p. 8.

[48] Not to be confused with impossible suicide. See VI note 76.

[49] Where the hopes themselves, or the unremitting nature of reality alone, are not absurd; the absurd is generated in the impossible relationship that is established between them. See: Camus. *The Myth of Sisyphus*. p. 24.

[50] 'You describe [this world] to me and you teach me to classify it. You enumerate its laws and in my thirst for knowledge I admit that they are true. You take apart its mechanism and my hope increases. At the final stage you teach me that this wondrous and multi-coloured universe can be reduced to the atom and that the atom itself can be reduced to the electron. All this is good and I wait for you to continue. But you tell me of an invisible planetary system in which electrons gravitate around a nucleus. You explain this world to me with an image. I realize then that you have been reduced to poetry: I shall never know. Have I the time to become indignant? You have already changed theories. So that science that was to teach me everything ends up in a hypothesis, that lucidity founders in metaphor, that uncertainty is resolved in a work of art' (Camus. *The Myth of Sisyphus*. pp. 16-7.).

[51] Camus. *The Myth of Sisyphus*. p. 28.

[52] Camus. *The Myth of Sisyphus*. p. 25.

[53] Camus. *The Myth of Sisyphus*. pp. 38-9.

[54] Camus. *The Myth of Sisyphus*. p. 40.

[55] Camus. *The Myth of Sisyphus*. p. 42.

[56] Camus. *The Myth of Sisyphus*. p. 50.

[57] Camus. *The Myth of Sisyphus*. p. 88.

[58] The charge made in: Solomon. *Dark Feelings, Grim Thoughts*.

[59] Camus. *The Myth of Sisyphus*. p. 25.

Printed in May 2021
by Rotomail Italia S.p.A., Vignate (MI) - Italy